I0616414

H!ITG!

HEY

AS SEEN ON TV | AS SEEN ON FILM

IT'S THAT GUY!

THE FAMETRACKER.COM GUIDE TO
CHARACTER ACTORS

TARA ARIANO and
ADAM STERNBERGH

QUIRK BOOKS
PHILADELPHIA

Library of Congress Cataloging in Publication Data. Available upon request.

ISBN: 1-59474-042-9

Printed in Singapore

Designed by Paul Kepple and Jude Buffum @ Headcase Design
www.headcasedesign.com

Edited by Erin Slonaker

Distributed in North America by Chronicle Books
85 Second Street
San Francisco, CA 94105

10 9 8 7 6 5 4 3 2 1

Quirk Books
215 Church Street
Philadelphia, PA 19106
www.quirkbooks.com

CONTENTS

FOREWORD

Not for nothing did we make Tobolowsky a charter member of our H!ITG! Hall of Fame. His movies have ranged from smash comedies (he played Ned Ryerson, the persistently annoying salesman in Groundhog Day*) to cult indie thrillers (Sammy Jankis in* Memento*). So we decided to ask him what makes a H!ITG! tick.*

So how did you get started in acting?

I was interested in acting from when I was a little, little kid. But back then, I thought that being an actor meant I'd have adventure in my life—I'd fight dinosaurs and fly rocket ships. What it really meant is that I'd sit in a trailer and do absolutely nothing for most of my life.

Did you act a lot as a kid?

In elementary school, I was in plays. In high school, I was in thespian contests. In college, I was named outstanding undergraduate theater student. All my life, I'd won acting awards—I was always considered one of the best of my group. I always say it's a lot like athletics: All the guys who are professional ballplayers, whether they start every game or are on the bench, all of them, for their entire lives, were the starring ballplayers on their little league teams.

What was your big break?

My biggest breakthrough was probably Alan Parker casting me as Clayton Townley, head of the Ku Klux Klan, in *Mississippi Burning*. Right after that, I did five films in a row.

CONTENTS

FOREWORD

A Q&A WITH STEPHEN TOBOLOWSKY

Not for nothing did we make Tobolowsky a charter member of our H!ITG! Hall of Fame. His movies have ranged from smash comedies (he played Ned Ryerson, the persistently annoying salesman in Groundhog Day*) to cult indie thrillers (Sammy Jankis in* Memento*). So we decided to ask him what makes a H!ITG! tick.*

So how did you get started in acting?

I was interested in acting from when I was a little, little kid. But back then, I thought that being an actor meant I'd have adventure in my life—I'd fight dinosaurs and fly rocket ships. What it really meant is that I'd sit in a trailer and do absolutely nothing for most of my life.

Did you act a lot as a kid?

In elementary school, I was in plays. In high school, I was in thespian contests. In college, I was named outstanding undergraduate theater student. All my life, I'd won acting awards—I was always considered one of the best of my group. I always say it's a lot like athletics: All the guys who are professional ballplayers, whether they start every game or are on the bench, all of them, for their entire lives, were the starring ballplayers on their little league teams.

What was your big break?

My biggest breakthrough was probably Alan Parker casting me as Clayton Townley, head of the Ku Klux Klan, in *Mississippi Burning*. Right after that, I did five films in a row.

Now you've done nearly one hundred films, and over a hundred TV appearances. You've done as many as six or seven films in one year. How do you fit it all in?

I have a manager who helps work out the schedules. I did *Where the Day Takes You* and *Basic Instinct* in the same week—one on Monday and one on Wednesday and Thursday. Several years ago, I got four movies in one day. I was jumping up and down, I was so excited.

Do people on the street recognize you a lot?

It happens several times a day, believe it or not.

Trust us—we believe it.

I find there are three categories of recognition. Category one: "It's Ned! It's Ned Ryerson!" Or, occasionally, *Sneakers*, or occasionally *Memento*. Category two: People who recognize me as an actor but don't have the foggiest idea what movie it was, so they start listing every movie they've ever seen, that I've never been in. They say, "Was it *Sister Act 2*?" "No." "Okay, don't tell me, don't tell me. Was it *Jeepers Creepers*?" "No." Category three: These are people who are certain they know me, not as an actor, but as someone from their past. I was in the Bahamas once, and someone mistook me for their insurance salesman. I was in Canada, and they mistook me for someone they played hockey with in high school. Some people think I was their history teacher.

Do you have a copy of each one of your films on a shelf in your house? Are there posters covering every wall?

No, nothing like that. What I did do, though, is one day when I was waiting in my trailer, I thought, Let me see if I can remember everything I've done. I think I came up with about 80 titles. In the beginning, yes, I would throw huge parties: "Hey, I'm playing Hotel Clerk in *Crazy Like a Fox*!" I'd have twelve of my best friends over and they'd all clap when I came on and said my three lines. But now, people mention stuff to me all the time that I don't remember. I probably haven't seen at least half of what I've been in.

As a character actor, you get to play so many different roles, where if you're Brad Pitt, you only get to play Brad Pitt.

When you have your name in front of the title, like Jim Carrey or Harrison Ford, the whole movie is about you. And everything about your character is on the page—your strengths, your weaknesses, your loves, your hates are all part of the plot of the film. But when you play the parts that I play, or other character actors play, those decisions and ideas aren't in the film. You have to be much more of a detective. You have to do much more work off the page to make it come to life.

Are there any roles you missed out on or passed on that you regret?

This is a complex question. My wife's theory is that it's all train tracks—you miss one track, then you're just on another track, and it's still good. For example, I missed out on playing Al, the Tool Time guy, on *Home Improvement*. They offered that role to me, but I turned it down. They could only guarantee one episode's salary, and they weren't going to let me do movies. And I had a baby coming, and I couldn't take that chance. Of course, it would have been millions and millions of dollars. But if I'd accepted that, I'd have missed out on *Groundhog Day*, *Thelma & Louise*, *Memento*—I wouldn't have my career. I wouldn't be where I am today. And I'm very happy to be where I am.

How do you explain your success?

I have a formula. To be a character actor, and make an impact, you need three things: You have to be good, in a movie that's good, that people have seen. You can be great in a terrible movie that no one sees, and they won't remember. Or if you're bad in a good movie that everyone sees, they won't remember. But if you're good, in a good movie, and people see it, then they remember.

HEY! IT'S THAT KEY TO THE ICONS!

AS SEEN ON TV
Stars or frequently guest-stars on TV series

DOUBLE THREAT
In addition to acting, practices another career

PERIOD PIECE
Frequently appears in films set in the past or future

AWARD NOMINEE
Nominated for, but has yet to win, an acting award

FOREIGN
Is or plays characters from mysterious, faraway lands

POSSE MEMBER
Works often with the same director and cast

AWARD WINNER
Recipient of an acting or other show business award

GRADUATE
Has achieved fame sufficient to outgrow H!ITG! status

STRAIGHT-TO-VIDEO
Shines in films that do not enjoy theatrical release

BALD
Has experienced significant visible hair loss

HALL OF FAME
Belongs in the pantheon of greatest H!ITG!s

TRIPLE THREAT
In addition to acting, practices two other careers

CANADIAN
Passes as American, but hails from the Great White North

ICONIC ROLE
Identified by one particularly memorable performance

UNGRADUATE
Once-famous actor whose star has fallen to H!ITG! status

DECEASED
Works much less since leaving this world for the next

MULTI-ETHNIC
Can portray a range of different racial backgrounds

VILLAIN
Often portrays nefarious characters

DISTINCTIVE FACIAL HAIR
Identified by trademark beard, mustache, or sideburns

NEW SCHOOL
Is part of the generation of up-and-coming H!ITG!s

WIG/PROSTHESIS USE
Is frequently disguised by false physical features

HEY!
IT'S THIS BOOK!

Sure, we all love the pretty people. What's not to love? For one thing, pretty people are fun to look at. That's why they're so perfect for the movies—in fact, every film should have at least two or three of them: a guy and a girl to kiss each other and another guy to get jealous about it.

But we're not here to celebrate the pretty people, who, let's face it, get celebrated enough already. We're here to toast the unknown, the overlooked, the underrated, and the often unnamed. The ones who never get their names over the title or their faces on *People* magazine. They don't get the big trailers or back end percentage of the gross. And they're never, ever the stars of the film: They're the ones who try to screw over the star in a land deal, or give him six weeks of detention, or save her life with tricky brain surgery, or have him whacked for that insolent remark, or make her stay and work Saturdays to finish that overdue report, or move in as his really annoying roommate who leaves half a grilled cheese sandwich between the couch cushions.

You probably don't even know their names, but you'd know them if you saw them. At Fametracker.com, we call them "Hey, It's That Guy!" (or Gal!), though through cinematic history they've also been known variously as "That Guy" or "What's-Her-Face" or "Whosamawhatzit" or "You know, the woman who always plays the annoying secretary" or "That scary guy from *Con Air* with all the tattoos." (Whose name is Danny Trejo, by the way; see page 124.)

And so, this volume is humbly dedicated to Danny Trejo and Jeffrey Jones (page 172) and Edie McClurg (page 176) and Viola Davis (page 131) and Stephen Tobolowsky (pages 7 and 153) and Ron Rifkin (page 74) and on and on—all the actors without whom Hollywood may as well shut its fancy cameras down for good. Because without these stalwarts, where would Hollywood be? Stuck making a bunch of movies in which pretty people walk around empty towns that have no sheriffs, no mayors, no busybody neighbors, no ineffectual high school principals, no bedraggled homicide detectives, no Mafia wiseguys, no loco gang members, no inbred hillbillies, and no sword-wielding Asian assassins—that's where. And we can all agree, that's a pretty boring movie, in a pretty boring town.

In assembling this guide, we've taken the most notable of the unnoted, the most worthy of the underrecognized. We've grouped them together in their natural habitats (the hospital, the government, the gentlemen's club, and more) and identified them by their primary characteristics; for example, That Brilliant but High-Strung Foreign Psychologist or That Ruddy, Intense Government Operative or That Wizened, Slightly Crazed, Chinatown-Dwelling Guru.

"But wait a second!" you might exclaim. "My favorite character actor [insert name here or, if unsure of name, insert rough physical description and two or three sample movies you're pretty sure he or she has been in] doesn't only play ruddy government operatives! Didn't you see [insert obscure straight-to-video-film you watched once]! She was brilliant in that!"

Yes, of course we saw that film, and yes, she was quite good. We aren't suggesting, by classifying the actors' types, that they've never played a different type of character in the past or they're incapable of doing so in the future. We're simply pointing out their hard-won niche—the very thing that makes them a candidate for *Hey! It's That Guy!* in the first place. Do we think Al Leong (page 120) is only capable of playing Dastardly Asian Killers, Terrorists, or Sidekicks with Fu Manchu Mustaches? Of course we don't. Would we like to see him play, say, a funny, non-nunchuck-wielding photographer more often, as he did in *She's Having a Baby*? Of course we would. Is it true that he's carved out a very fine career playing killers, terrorists, and deadly sidekicks—as he did in *Die Hard*, when he played that guy with the machine gun who eats the chocolate bar from the candy case? Yes, it is true. We love him for it, and, we suspect, so do you. Though you might not know it yet.

So how do you become a Hey! It's That Guy!? Well, it's pretty simple. Number one, you have to be in a lot of movies. Number two, it helps if you usually play exactly the same kind of role. Number three, you can't have a high name-recognition factor among the general public: For example, Philip Baker Hall (page 94) is in, but William H. Macy, a one-time proud H!ITG!, is now out. (Oscar nominations will do that to you.) Philip Seymour Hoffman (page 57) is on the cusp, for now. You know who we mean, right? The guy from *Magnolia* and *The Talented Mr. Ripley*. Great actor, kind of portly? Yeah, that guy.

And to that guy and all the guys and all the gals, we say thank you. Thank you for helping to make great movies great, good movies better, and bad movies watchable. (And when you're a H!ITG!, you're going to be in a lot of bad movies. It's just unavoidable.) Thank you for playing all the thankless roles. And thank you, most of all, for showing us ourselves. Because, in the end, the reason we love the H!ITG!s so very, very much is because all of us in the audience innately understand that if it were us up there, that's who we'd be, too. We can love the stars, but it's the people just behind them—and to the left—that we truly relate to. The teachers. The lawyers. The bartenders. The grating coworkers. The gossipy neighbors. The ice-blooded, possibly psychotic CIA agents who can kill you fifteen different ways with a bulldog clip and a Post-It.

Okay, maybe not that last guy. But we could definitely be the teacher. Maybe even the grating coworker. That much we know for sure.

A TRIBUTE TO J. T. WALSH:

The Hey! It's That Guy! section of Fametracker.com is the Bizarro World of fame—where one's renown is determined not on the basis of who can land the most leading roles and get on the most magazine covers, but on the basis of who can disappear the most thoroughly into pivotal character roles, so that we know them not by their given names, but by their memorable, if anonymous, performances.

It is here that the late J. T. Walsh is not mourned, but celebrated, as the patron saint of Hey! It's That Guy!s. It's the reason you'll hear us mention him from time to time—we can't help but compare more current Hey! It's That Guy!s to the original. Walsh isn't the ultimate Hey! It's That Guy! because of a prolific oeuvre; he had fewer than half the credits of, for instance, his colleague Seymour Cassel. Nor is Walsh remembered for the dizzying range of his performances, like J. K. Simmons, or for his prodigious acting talent, like Philip Seymour Hoffman. J. T. Walsh played the usual H!ITG! roles—cops, army guys, politicians—and he played them all more or less the same. But what he did, he did so well. With each new role, the audience fell in hate with him again as if for the first time.

The whole reason the Hey! It's That Guy! classification exists is because not every role in a movie or TV show can be the hero, or the villain, or even the scene-stealing boob. You need actors to play the characters in the background, and to do that well—to do it so well that, even if you appreciate their work, you have no desire to learn more about them personally, or even find out their names.

Throughout his life, that was J. T. Walsh: reliable yet modest, talented yet anonymous. He embodied what Hey! It's That Guy!-ing is all about.

Atten-hut! You're in the army now! And you know what that means? First of all, you'll be humiliated by a relentless drill sergeant with a bullhorn voice, who won't consider his job finished until either you're crying, you've quit, or you've blown your brains out. If you survive that, you'll no doubt be assigned to some chickenshit outfit in which your tough but noble sergeant is always being overridden by a supercilious higher-up, whose only concern is advancing

HEY! IT'S CHAPTER ONE:
THE ARMY

his own career and who doesn't know what it's like down here, man! In the trenches! But you know, because you'll be in the trenches, or perhaps in a foxhole, probably next to a yammering, overbearing yahoo who'll make you miss the nuanced politics of the drill sergeant. Then, at night, as you shiver in the dark, you'll find solace by confiding in the grinning, soulful tough guy, who's seen some crazy shit go down.

Adam Baldwin

Stats: **AS SEEN ON TV**

HEY! IT'S THAT
TOWERING TOUGH!

ICONIC ROLE

1980 was a very good year for Adam Baldwin. In that year, he starred in one of the most touching, influential, and seminal motion pictures of this or any age. Oh, and he also appeared in *Ordinary People*.

Sure, *Ordinary People* won the Oscar for Best Picture, but the real triumph for Adam Baldwin in 1980 was his role as Ricky Linderman in *My Bodyguard*. For those of you who haven't seen this film, Baldwin played a hulking loner who's retained by Chris Makepeace, a spindly nerd, to protect him from Moody, a vicious school bully (played by a then unknown and too-young-to-shave Matt Dillon).

Since then, Baldwin's been busy doing two things: 1) Playing a string of nameless, towering toughs (he is 6'4", after all) in movies such as *Full Metal Jacket*, *Predator 2*, *Wyatt Earp*, and *Independence Day*, as well as appearing in countless lesser efforts (and you know we're veering into sketchy territory when we talk about "lesser efforts" than *Predator 2*) such as *Cold Sweat*, *Deadbolt*, and *Sawbones*; and 2) convincing people that he's not one of the Baldwin brothers. Because he's not. Seriously. It's Alec, Stephen, Billy, Daniel, Tito, Donnie, Ryan, "Ace," Stretchy, and Kip. No Adam.

Ordinary People Stillman **1980**	*Full Metal Jacket* Animal Mother **1987**	*Firefly* Jayne Cobb **2002–2003**
My Bodyguard Ricky Linderman **1980**	*The X Files* Knowle Rohrer **2001–2002**	

Keith David

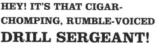

HEY! IT'S THAT CIGAR-CHOMPING, RUMBLE-VOICED DRILL SERGEANT!

AS SEEN ON TV

AWARD NOMINEE

According to legend, Keith David's first dramatic role was as the Cowardly Lion in a grade-school production of ***The Wizard of Oz***. Which is ironic, given that David has likely never acted cowardly again the rest of his life. With his deep, rumbling voice and hulking presence, David is born to intimidate.

David proved his snarly credentials early, as the tough-talking, snow-encrusted Childs in John Carpenter's ***The Thing*** and then, four years later, as the snarly-but-sympathetic soldier King in ***Platoon***. (Between those two gigs, he spent a few years as "Keith the Southwood Carpenter" on ***Mister Rogers' Neighborhood***, in which we're guessing he was neither tough talking nor snarly.) He sometimes gets to play against type, as when he appeared as Cameron Diaz's stepdad in ***There's Something About Mary***—though even there, he was a wee bit snarly and intimidating; at least until he saw Ben Stiller's wing-ding snaggled up in his zipper.

Even if you've only seen him a few times, it's easy to picture David's trademark gap-toothed grin—which always seems to have a half-chewed cigar butt floating around in it somewhere. In fact, we like to imagine that little baby Keith was born with a cigar already in his mouth. Then he pulled it out, spat, and told his dad to drop and give him twenty.

They Live!
Frank
1988

Requiem for a Dream
Big Tim
2000

Agent Cody Banks
C.I.A. Director
2002

Dead Presidents
Kirby
1995

Barbershop
Lester Wallace
2002

John Diehl

Stats:

HEY! IT'S THAT UNREMARKABLE
ARMY GUY!

There are a lot of people in the army. Not just the maverick lieutenant who goes with his gut and nearly gets his whole platoon killed. Not just the aged, corrupt general who lost his way somewhere along the line and winds up putting on his dress uniform, looking at himself in the mirror, saluting, and then blowing his brains out. No, there are other people in the military— the guys who give terse speeches, the guys who follow orders, the guys who shout things like, "I expect you to follow orders!"

John Diehl is that man in the background: the lesser of two lawyers at a trial, the army guy who doesn't kill himself but who discovers the guy who killed himself and then writes a report on it. Given his role as Det. Larry Zito in the too-cool-for-school '80s cop drama *Miami Vice*, it's surprising that Diehl wound up mostly playing straight-laced army men, crisply efficient attorneys, and other necessary but largely unmemorable apparatchiks. His post–*Miami Vice* highlight is probably his turn as G. Gordon Liddy in Oliver Stone's *Nixon*. He also played Joe DiMaggio in a made-for-TV movie about the Rat Pack. This is the Hey! It's That Guy!'s lot in life: playing minor tertiary roles, interrupted occasionally by semi-star-turns as historical figures they sort of resemble.

Miami Vice
Det. Larry Zito
1984–1987

Nixon
G. Gordon Liddy
1995

Pearl Harbor
Senior Doctor
2001

Stargate
Maj. Charles Kawalsky
1994

Con Air
Public Defender
1997

R. Lee Ermey

Stats: **AWARD NOMINEE**

HEY! IT'S THAT LOUD, ANGRY, BELITTLING, HARD-ASSED
DRILL SERGEANT!

VILLAIN

PERIOD PIECE

As Gunnery Sgt. Hartman in Stanley Kubrick's 1987 movie **Full Metal Jacket**, R. Lee Ermey provides the least romantic portrayal of army service in film. Hartman's great at the part of drill sergeanting where he destroys the soldier's sense of individuality and will to live; he's less good at the part where he's supposed to build up the soldier's self-esteem again by making him appreciate his part within the team. Or so he realizes when Pvt. Leonard Lawrence (Vincent D'Onofrio) cracks under Hartman's relentless abuse and commits a spectacular suicide.

Now Ermey always plays mean army guys. He plays army guys in movies and TV shows about the army (**China Beach**). He plays army guys in movies and TV shows not about the army (**Civil Wars**). He plays the *ghosts* of army guys (**The Frighteners**). Even when only his voice is called for, he plays army guys (**Toy Story** and **Toy Story 2**, **The Simpsons**). He occasionally mixes it up by playing a mean cop, but it's still basically the same credit: Sheriff. Marine. General. Colonel. Coach. Captain. Lieutenant. Even when he tosses in a senator or president or secretary of state, it's the same role: He's tough. He's irascible. He'll spit in your face as soon as look at you, son!

Toy Soldiers General Kramer **1991**	*Prefontaine* Bill Bowerman **1997**	*The Texas Chainsaw Massacre* Sheriff Hoyt **2003**
	Dead Man Walking Clyde Percy **1995**	*Recess: School's Out* Col. O'Malley **2001**

Michael Ironside

Stats:

AS SEEN ON TV

BALD

CANADIAN

HEY! IT'S THAT HOMICIDAL
ROGUE COLONEL!

Is there any actor with a more appropriate name than Michael Ironside? The only way his name could be more fitting is if it was Michael Chillingglare or Michael Crushyournuts.

Michael Ironside looks like a pocket Jack Nicholson. But where Nicholson is equal parts intensity and mischief, Ironside is equal parts intensity and intensity. He's the glowering killer from *Total Recall* who scrambled all over Earth and Mars to put a slug in Schwarzenegger's back. He's the coldhearted boat owner in *The Perfect Storm*, pushing men out into the angry, towering troughs. (Note to boat owners: If you find out Michael Ironside is playing you in a movie, you're probably not going to be portrayed as a convivial fop.) He's the chilling assassin in the David Cronenberg classic *Scanners*, about people who murder other people by making their heads explode. Ironside's played good guys, too—most famously Lt. Cmdr. Rick "Jester" Heatherly in *Top Gun* and Lt. Jean Rasczak in *Starship Troopers*—but even his good guys are frighteningly intense.

That's a pretty good description of Michael Ironside. He could probably kill you just by being so intense that he makes your head explode. And if that doesn't work, he'll use his fists. Or whatever's handy.

Extreme Prejudice
Maj. Paul Hackett
1987

Major Payne
Lt. Col. Stone
1995

ER
Dr. Swift
1995–1998

Total Recall
Richter
1990

SeaQuest DSV
Capt. Oliver Hudson
1995–1996

Zeljko Ivanek

HEY! IT'S THAT SUPERCILIOUS
APPARATCHIK!

First of all, according to "Jess's Zeljko Ivanek Page" Web site, the name is pronounced "Zhel-ko Eve-anek" with the *zh* sounding like the z in the word *azure*. Secondly, yes, there really is a "Jess's Zeljko Ivanek Page" Web site.

You may know Zeljko Ivanek as the scheming troll of a governor, James Devlin, on HBO's *Oz*, or as the slimy weasel of a lawyer who tormented Alex Kingston on *ER*. Or you may recognize him as Cordell, the kowtowing manservant to Mason Verger in *Hannibal*, or as Harrell, the vaguely-weaselly-but-not-that-bad guy-in-the-helicopter-giving-directions who gets Tom Sizemore lost in *Black Hawk Down*.

The point is, if you know Zeljko Ivanek, then there's a good chance you know him as a scheming, ambitious, amoral bureaucrat who's eager to slip a shiv into anyone who blocks his scrambling climb to success. He doesn't get to play the general; he plays the general's efficient aide. His brand of evil isn't a chaotic, out-of-control, I-am-a-destroyer-of-world evilness, but a thin-lipped, efficient, let's-get-this-done-and-move-on-to-the-next-item-on-the-evil-agenda evilness.

Zeljko Ivanek is a bureaucrat of evil. He's an evilcrat.

Homicide: Life on the Street	*Donnie Brasco*	*The Manchurian Candidate*
A.S.A. Ed Danvers	Tim Curley	Vaughn Utly
1993–1999	**1997**	**2004**

Courage Under Fire	*Unfaithful*
Banacek, General's Aide	Det. Dean
1996	**2002**

David Keith

HEY! IT'S THAT STEELY-EYED
SOUTHERN OFFICER!

AWARD NOMINEE

If you remember David Keith from *An Officer and a Gentleman* and *Lords of Discipline* back in the 1980s, then you know there was a time when his steely Southern charm had positioned him as a promising leading man. So what happened? Answer: 1) Patrick Swayze and 2) Keith David.

In fact, it's easy to imagine an alternate fate for David Keith, in which he went on to play a rough-hewn dance teacher in *Dirty Dancing*, that run-away sleeper hit. He might then have parlayed that notoriety into a role in, say, *Ghost*, in which he haunts his former wife in a dubiously romantic attempt to convince her not to get on with her life, but rather to pine for her dead husband forever in perpetual misery.

But he did not star in those movies. Instead, he went on to star in *Off and Running*, *Caged Fear*, and *Whose Child Is This? The War for Baby Jessica*. Because his veritable doppelganger, Patrick Swayze, had by that time effectively elbowed him out of the spotlight.

And then there's Keith David.

Keith David is the burly black character actor from *Pitch Black* and *There's Something About Mary* who is profiled on page 17. When you're juggling both a veritable doppelganger and another character actor with the flippity-flop version of your name—well, that's a lot of sandbags strung to the hot air balloon of your career.

The Great Santini Red Petus **1979**	*The Lords of Discipline* Will **1983**	*Behind Enemy Lines* Master Chief Tom O'Malley **2001**

An Officer and a Gentleman Sid Worley **1982**	*U-571* Maj. Matthew Coonan **2000**

John C. McGinley

AS SEEN ON TV

PERIOD PIECE

HEY! IT'S THAT
HIGH-STRUNG, OFFICIOUS
LIEUTENANT!

John C. McGinley must drink a lot of coffee.

Otherwise, how to explain it? Protein powders? Uppers? Alien metabolism? Just think of the energy it must require to remain Hollywood's go-to high-strung jerk for two decades—which is what McGinley's done, since he first seared himself into our collective memories as the villainous brown-noser Sergeant Red O'Neill in 1986's *Platoon*.

You'd think he'd mix in the occasional role as "Mellow Head-Shop Owner" or "Laidback Surf Shack Attendant," just to give the veins in his forehead a rest. But no! He's soldiered on with one memorable, wigged-out jackass after another, from Agent Harp in *Point Break* to Marine Captain Hendrix in *The Rock* to consultant Bob Slydell in *Office Space* and Sergeant Sisk in *The Animal*. Then he didn't take a rest—he went the other way! He said, "You think this is hard? I can do this every week!" and started his lauded gig as the obnoxious Dr. Perry Cox on NBC's *Scrubs*.

As a result, McGinley has worked a ton in his career, carved out an exceptional niche for himself, and established an unusually faithful fan base for a guy who's quintessentially a character actor. As far as Hey! It's That Guy!s go, he's about as good as it gets.

Or, as he might say, He's! About! As! Good! As! It! Gets!

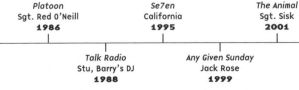

Platoon	Se7en	The Animal
Sgt. Red O'Neill	California	Sgt. Sisk
1986	**1995**	**2001**

Talk Radio	Any Given Sunday
Stu, Barry's DJ	Jack Rose
1988	**1999**

Joe Morton

Stats: AS SEEN ON TV

HEY! IT'S THAT NOBLE,
DUTIFUL SOLDIER!

ICONIC ROLE

PERIOD PIECE

Because movies are often written by the kind of comfortable, privileged, draft-dodging wusses who end up in Hollywood, they seldom present an appealing image of service in the armed forces. Army guys on film are usually screaming, authoritarian psychos in the R. Lee Ermey (page 19) mold; three-dimensional military characters—sometimes conflicted about their service, but striving every day to honor the countries they represent—are rare. This latter kind is the sort of army guy Joe Morton plays.

Virtually every Joe Morton character is the portrait of integrity, nobility, and rectitude. He is dignified and dutiful as Col. Delmore Payne in John Sayles's *Lone Star*. But there's not all that much difference between his serene wisdom as a career officer and his serene wisdom as a cinnamon-candy-offering psychiatrist (*What Lies Beneath*) or an amazingly tolerant advertising executive (*Bounce*) or a Supreme Court Justice (*Mutiny*) or the lawyer for a fictional militant African-American activist group (a recurring guest role on *Law & Order*).

Our favorite kind of Morton role is the noble scientist. In *Terminator 2: Judgment Day* and in several episodes of the WB drama *Smallville*, Morton plays brilliant men whose intellectual gifts are put to nefarious use by unscrupulous bastards. Marching forward in doomed causes controlled by powers far above him, Joe Morton is always a good soldier.

The Brother from Another Planet   *The Walking Dead*   *The Astronaut's Wife*
The Brother   Sgt. Barkley   Sherman Reese, NASA Representative
1984   **1995**   **1999**

Speed   *Executive Decision*
Lt. Herb "Mac" McMahon   Sgt. "Cappy" Matheny
1994   **1996**

Leland Orser

Stats:

HEY! IT'S THAT KNOCK-KNEED
DESERTER!

Ask not for whom Leland Orser's knees are knocking. They knock for thee. Leland Orser seems, by all available evidence, to be a genial, confident, and not unattractive chap. Shave Orser's head, however, and strap a pair of wire-framed glasses on him, and you've got yourself one convincingly jittery dweeb. Hand him a knife, and you've got a nicely agitated psycho. Orser is a veritable virtuoso of skittishness. If knocking knees were the cello, he'd be Yo-Yo Ma.

You may have heard those knees a-knockin' during such classic Orser performances as Purvis, an ill-fated and extremely nervous gent in *Alien: Resurrection*. Or perhaps you recall him as Crazed Man in Massage Parlour in *Se7en*. He also acted all sweaty and nervous and skittish as Charles in the very bad movie *Very Bad Things*. Generally speaking, you can bet that any Leland Orser role will involve some combination of sweating, stammering, darting eyes, and jumping at loud sounds.

Orser's filled the rest of his time with the usual Hey! It's That Guy! journeyman work: a lieutenant in *Saving Private Ryan* here, a major in *Pearl Harbor* there. He makes a pretty good army guy, assuming there's call for a nerdy army guy who can't stand the sound of explosions, which every celluloid army seems to need at least one of.

Independence Day Tech/Medical Assistant #1 **1996**	*Confidence* Lionel Dolby **2003**	*Runaway Jury* Lamb **2003**

Alien: Resurrection Purvis **1997**	*Daredevil* Wesley Owen Welch **2003**

Daniel von Bargen

HEY! IT'S THAT DISAPPOINTED
MILITARY MAN!

A sampling of Daniel von Bargen's résumé, by role:

- General (four times)
- Sheriff (four times)
- Lieutenant (twice)
- Commandant (in a recurring TV role)
- Chief (five times)
- Detective (three times)
- Commander (once)
- Sergeant (once)
- Warden (once)
- Captain (once)
- Officer (once) and, finally,
- Douglas MacArthur (once)

The man's been typecast, is what we're saying. This niche might have worked out just fine for von Bargen had he turned up only as secondary and tertiary characters in forgettable movies like ***The General's Daughter***, ***G.I. Jane***, and ***Universal Soldier: The Return***. But then von Bargen surfaced as Commandant Edwin Spangler, Francis's headmaster on the Fox sitcom ***Malcolm in the Middle***, and now when he shows up in military uniform—

Seinfeld
Kruger
1997–1998

Broken Arrow
Air Force Gen. Creely
1996

Truman
Gen. Douglas MacArthur
1995

The West Wing
Air Force Gen. Ken Shannon
1999

even without the hook and eyepatch—on ***The West Wing***, instead of thinking, "Who is this military advisor, and what is he going to tell the president?" the viewer wonders, "What is Spangler doing on NBC?"

Ironically, Spangler represents the most nuanced army guy on von Bargen's CV. At the military school, Spangler is strict but generally fair, eccentric but not unbalanced. Spangler is scared of the Alabama townie girls who set upon his young charges, intrigued by the gay rodeo when it comes to town, affectionate toward his pet dog. Most memorably, Spangler nursed a brief crush on Francis's mother Lois (played by Jane Kaczmarek) when she came to visit Francis at school. In his efforts to ingratiate himself to Lois, Spangler evinces a tender ennui that perhaps he'd chosen the wrong path in life—one that had led him away from women as magnetic and scary as Lois. If nothing else, the sight of Spangler in his creamy cable-knit sweater was a glimpse into the man's seldom seen and oddly touching private life.

After his pivotal role in ***O Brother, Where Art Thou?*** as a satanic Southern sheriff, von Bargen might have vaulted up a character-actor tier, getting to play small-town doctors or leading ladies' sympathetic fathers as well as lawmen and army guys. Sadly, that didn't happen. But we'll always have Spangler.

0 Brother, Where Art Thou?
Sheriff Cooley/The Devil
2000

Super Troopers
Police Chief Bruce Grady
2001

Malcolm in the Middle
Commandant Edwin Spangler
2000

The Majestic
Federal Agent Ellerby
2001

You might not think that there are enough roles as hayseeds, inbreds, yokels, and menacing, snaggle-toothed mountain dwellers to sustain an actor's entire career. But you'd be wrong—so very wrong. Look, over there—it's the wild-eyed, buck-toothed banjo picker! Spooky, especially if you're from the city, or are for some reason frightened of the banjo! Don't run, though—you'll just fall right into the arms of that greasy bumpkin. He'd sure 'nuff like to skin y'all and throw you in a pot!

HEY! IT'S CHAPTER TWO:
THE BACKWOODS

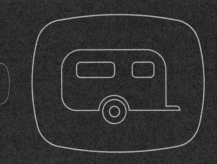

Thank goodness for the good ol' racist Southern sheriff: fat, mirrored shades, fond of hounds, likes to turn the hose on newcomers. He'll protect you, as long as you're white. Given these persistent stereotypes, one might get the impression that Hollywood's not too fond of our hillbilly brethren. In fact, hillbillies have every reason to be hoppin' mad. Then again, they're too drunk on moonshine to get the truck off the blocks and drive to the theater to see a movie anyway.

Joe Don Baker

HEY! IT'S THAT BUTT-WHUPPIN'
SOUTHERN LAWMAN!

To a certain generation, Joe Don Baker was a bona fide movie star—a kind of bacon-wrapped Brando who shot to fame as Buford Pusser in the 1973 hit **Walking Tall**. We, it should be said, are not of that generation. We are of a later generation, one that was not yet walking, tall or otherwise, when *Walking Tall* was released.

So we remember the Joe Don Baker of the late '70s and early '80s, a time during which Joe Don owned—not rented, not leased, but *owned*—the part of bad-ass lawman in every hicksploitation flick that rambled down the dirt road. Which, of course, makes him no less of a movie star in our books.

From Chief Earl M. Eischied (**To Kill a Cop**) and Deputy Sheriff Thomas Jefferson Geronimo III (**Final Justice**) to Chief Karlin (**Fletch**) and Sheriff Onstad (**The Abduction of Kari Swenson**), there was no actor better at capturing the spirit of the laconic, possibly or obviously corrupt, definitely shit-kicking, good ol' boy cop than our man, Joe to the Don to the Baker. And for some reason, in the 1970s, America was obsessed with shit-kicking Southerners,

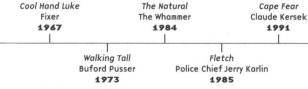

Cool Hand Luke
Fixer
1967

The Natural
The Whammer
1984

Cape Fear
Claude Kersek
1991

Walking Tall
Buford Pusser
1973

Fletch
Police Chief Jerry Karlin
1985

from *The Dukes of Hazzard* to *Smokey and the Bandit*. Which meant that Joe Don Baker was never at a loss for work.

He hasn't disappeared since; far from it, in fact. He's shown up in ***Reality Bites*** and ***Congo*** and ***Mars Attacks!*** and ***Tomorrow Never Dies***, usually as porcine dads or CIA agents or other slow-witted authority figures. And, truth be told, Joe Don spent much of his life playing cartoon versions of that first, famous, *Walking Tall* character, which wasn't exactly Hamlet to begin with. And while we can see the wisdom of casting Burt Reynolds—the original Bandit—as Boss Hogg in the tongue-in-cheek 2005 remake of *The Dukes of Hazzard*, we can't help but feel a little peeved that they didn't put a call in to the Don—the Joe Don, that is.

Because no one can dispute the fact that, if there were a Mount Rushmore of Hey! It's That Guy!s, his grizzled mug would be chiseled on it. To paraphrase Michael Jackson: We want to love you, JDB.

Reality Bites Tom Pierce **1994**	*Mars Attacks!* Richie's Dad **1996**	*Joe Dirt* Don **2001**
Congo R. B. Travis, TraviCom CEO **1995**	*Tomorrow Never Dies* Jack Wade **1997**	

Patrick Cranshaw

Stats:

PERIOD PIECE

HEY! IT'S THAT CODGER, COOT, OR REALLY, REALLY OLD MAN!

Patrick Cranshaw, who was born in 1919, enjoyed his first screen credit in 1960, in a film titled **The Seventh Commandment**. But it wasn't until 1970 that he found his true calling. That year, he played Grandpa on **Green Acres**. In a later episode that same season, he played "Old Man."

He went on to appear in such TV hits as **The Bob Newhart Show**, **Mork & Mindy**, **Wonder Woman**, **Hunter**, **Quantum Leap**, and **Ooaah**, playing such characters as "Old Gentleman," "Old Man," "Codger," and Mr. Knickerbocker. He's also put the "silver" in "silver screen," playing such unforgettably aged roles as Grandfather, Grandpa, Gramps, "Man on Gurney," and "Man Dying in Elevator."

But wait. We know what you're thinking. What does he do in these films? Does he just stand around and . . . be *old*? Well, no. Quite often he stands around and is old, then makes a ribald remark or wrestles a naked woman. Because, you know, that's just funny.

All hail Patrick Cranshaw: King of the Codgers, Emperor of the Elderly, the Grand Poobah of Grand Old Coots.

Bonnie and Clyde
Bank teller (uncredited)
1967

The Hudsucker Proxy
Ancient Sorter
1994

Old School
Blue
2003

The Beverly Hillbillies
Reverend Mason
1993

Best in Show
Leslie Ward Cabot
2000

Brad Dourif

Stats: AWARD WINNER

VILLAIN

HEY! IT'S THAT CREEPY, SHADOW-LURKING COUNTRY DOCTOR!

Does the fine character actor Brad Dourif ever wonder what might have been had he not taken his second-ever movie role as mental-hospital patient Billy Bibbit in 1975's *One Flew Over the Cuckoo's Nest*? Because anyone who sees that Oscar-winning picture will always be haunted by his tender, crushing performance. And Brad Dourif will always be haunted by it, too.

Dourif is now the human equivalent of a bat flapping out of the shadows or a sudden sting of frantic string music: He makes things a bit creepier. When even your vocal chords are scary—Dourif provides the voice for the titular doll-cum-murderer in the *Chucky* films—then you know you've definitely got your creep on.

When he isn't playing weaselly weirdos like Chickie Levitt and Grima Wormtongue, Dourif—oddly—plays a lot of doctors. This must say something about our collective fear of the medical profession. Because Dourif isn't playing genial, hop-up-here-so-I-can-take-your-temperature-then-give-you-a-lollipop kinds of doctors. These are scary, stringy-haired, rusty-instrument-using, long-needle-unsheathing kinds of doctors. Even Doc Cochran, the Old West doctor he plays on HBO's *Deadwood*, while not unspeakably evil, is still . . . you know, off-putting.

One Flew Over the
Cuckoo's Nest
Billy Bibbit
1975

Dune
Piter De Vries
1984

Blue Velvet
Raymond
1986

Mississippi Burning
Dep. Clinton Pell
1988

The Lord of the Rings:
The Two Towers
Grima Wormtongue
2002

Charles Durning

HEY! IT'S THAT SWEATY, SEERSUCKER-WEARING
LAWYER!

Charles Durning has played Santa Claus in (to date) five unrelated Christmas-themed projects. Who's he going to be asked to play next—Howard Taft? Homer Simpson? Durning, we want you to live a good long life. Just because they comp you a steak at Morton's doesn't mean you have to eat it.

Whatever damage Durning's extra poundage may be doing to his organs, however, it's great for his career, as he has played every movie's default big, fat Southerner (that is, when he's not playing the default fat Italian or Irish cop, as in, respectively, *Dog Day Afternoon* and *Dick Tracy*) Durning was born to play characters with names like Otis P. Hazelrigg and Louis Thibodo and Wylie Hunnicutt. He is in his element as a folksy yet wily lawyer, sweltering in his shirtsleeves in a dim '30s-era Alabama courtroom. The guy who, after court, heads down to the ol' barber shop for a trim and a jaw and maybe a chaw. Then steps out in his summer-weight suit—white or

The Sting
Lt. William Snyder
1973

The Best Little Whorehouse in Texas
Governor
1982

Evening Shade
Dr. Harlan Elldridge
1990–1994

The Front Page
Murphy
1974

Tootsie
Les Nichols
1982

seersucker, preferably—and suspenders, to stand under some insufficient shade or perhaps sit in a rocker on a sun porch, fanning himself with a fedora and begging whatever woman is handy to bring him some lemonade.

Durning doesn't always play stereotypical Southern lawyers. He's also good at priests (as in his recurring role on *Everybody Loves Raymond*) and politicians. But really, all that's changed for Durning as he's aged is that he now plays more folksy judges than folksy attorneys. And when a Jim Henson project comes along, he's no longer spry enough to play the villain, as in *The Muppet Movie*; instead, he has to play someone who does a lot more sitting, and occasionally laughing, thus causing his belly to jiggle like a bowl full of jelly, as in *Elmo Saves Christmas*.

Jiggle on, sir. But you might consider—just once in a while—having the baked chicken instead of the fried.

HEY! IT'S CHAPTER TWO: THE BACKWOODS

The Hudsucker Proxy
Waring Hudsucker
1994

O Brother, Where Art Thou?
Pappy O'Daniel
2000

Rescue Me
Tommy's Dad
2004

Home for the Holidays
Henry Larson
1995

State and Main
Mayor George Bailey
2002

William Forsythe

HEY! IT'S THAT DIMWITTED
HAYSEED!

Dear William Forsythe,

    You sure don't look like a William Forsythe. You look more like an Ernest Paxton. Or maybe a Sergeant Buck Atwater. Or perhaps a Pigiron, or a Pug Face Crusher—names, each and every one, of characters you've played. As one might guess, these characters tend toward 1) dangerously amoral special agents; 2) bad-seed police officers; or 3) backward, inbred country boys.

    You are a fine character actor, William Forsythe—especially so as John Goodman's squealing, grinning sidekick in ***Raising Arizona***. But don't you know that actors named William Forsythe are supposed to be tall and distinguished, with silver-gray hair, and play captains of industry or the curmudgeonly old rich man in some Olsen twins movie? You know, the one who's constantly grimacing and shaking his fist as the Olsens run roughshod through the mansion before eventually discovering that he, too, is a kid at heart? Or perhaps you should be playing a character like, say, we don't know . . . Blake Carrington, the patriarch of *Dynasty*, as John Forsythe did?

The Man Who Wasn't There
Pug Face Crusher
1983

Raising Arizona
Evelle
1987

Dick Tracy
Flattop
1990

Once Upon a Time in America
Philip "Cockeye" Stein
1984

Extreme Prejudice
Buck Atwater
1987

John Forsythe—your father!

Yes, it's true, William Forsythe. You are the son of Blake Carrington. You are the son of the voice of Charlie on *Charlie's Angels*.

But let us tell you a little story, William Forsythe. Your father was actually born John Lincoln Freund. And he had the good sense to change his name to "John Forsythe" once it became apparent that he would become the kind of actor who spends his career playing distinguished, silver-haired characters—characters with names like Blake Carrington and Rex Roper and Reade Jamieson and Dr. Robert Kier.

So, rather than taking your father's name, you must take his example. You, too, must change your name to something more appropriate— something like Randy Braxton or Skip Knox or Buck Mullett—as it has become apparent that you will spend your career playing dimwitted hayseeds or menacing thugs or rogue cops.

We suggest Skip Knox.

HEY! IT'S CHAPTER TWO: THE BACKWOODS   37

The Untouchables
Al Capone
1993–1994

Virtuosity
William Cochran
1995

The Rock
Special Agent Ernest Paxton
1996

Deuce Bigalow: Male Gigolo
Det. Chuck Fowler
1999

Blue Streak
Hardcastle
1999

Courtney Gains

NEW SCHOOL

HEY! IT'S THAT
RED-HEADED GEEK!

"You shit on my house. You shit on my house!"

This line, spoken by Courtney Gains as Kenneth Wurman in **Can't Buy Me Love**, is inarguably the finest, fiercest slamming-Patrick-Dempsey-up-against-the-arcade-game line in his career.

Long story short: Dempsey had become popular by buying the affections of the school's most popular girl. Soon, through a combination of unfortunate circumstances and questionable choices, he found himself throwing shit at the house of his former best friend, Kenneth Wurman, the king of the high school nerds. And Wurman was having none of it.

So Wurman hoists Patrick Dempsey up against that arcade game and yells that pithy, memorable line, a line which, given the context, vibrates with near-Shakespearean resonance.

Courtney Gains has most often been stuck playing nerds, geeks, and misfits of all stripes, including the stripes that live in the mountains and call one of their cousins "Dad." But for one brief moment, nerds around the world could cheer, as Courtney Gains got all up in the grill of every lousy bastard who'd ever thrown metaphorical "shit" on our metaphorical "houses." And oh, how we cheered. Er, *they* cheered, we mean.

| *Children of the Corn*
Malachai
1984 | *Colors*
Whitey
1988 | *Sweet Home Alabama*
Wade
2002 |

Back to the Future
Mark Dixon
1985

Memphis Belle
Sgt. Eugene McVey
1990

Clint Howard

HEY! IT'S THAT ODDLY
MENACING MAN-BOY!

What you need to know about Clint Howard: Clint Howard is Ron Howard's brother. He has appeared in nearly all of Ron's movies.

Clint Howard has played the following characters: Rughead, Googie, Slinky, Bobo, Paco, Cheese, Nipples, Mr. Toothache, and "Rapist." From this list, we may deduce that Clint Howard does not look very much like Brad Pitt.

Clint Howard has also played Stalin. And Henrik Ibsen.

Clint Howard is sometimes confused with another very successful, long-time Hey! It's That Guy!, Michael J. Pollard (page 43), because both men often play odd little man-boys. Clint Howard, however, does not usually get cast as innocent man-boys in the way that Michael J. Pollard does, but rather as innocent-seeming but actually malevolent man-boys. He plays rapists and killers and, in one episode of *Seinfeld*, the Smog Strangler. In other words, Howard plays man-boys you don't want to mess with.

Clint Howard is kind of awesome.

Clint Howard received a Lifetime Achievement Award at the 1998 MTV Movie Awards, one of the very few things they have ever gotten right on the MTV Movie Awards.

Tango & Cash
Slinky
1989

Apollo 13
Sy Liebergot
1995

How the Grinch Stole Christmas
Whobris
2000

The Paper
Ray Blaisch
1994

The Waterboy
Paco
1998

O-Lan Jones

AS SEEN ON TV

HEY! IT'S THAT IGNORANT, MOUTH-BREATHING
HICK!

WIG/PROSTHESIS USE

VILLAIN

O-Lan Jones has the genetic misfortune of being born with gormless bug eyes, jutting buck teeth, and stringy hair. She plays hysterical, small-minded townspeople, quaint service-persons, and religious fundamentalists.

PERIOD PIECE

A frequent member of Tim Burton's ensemble casts, O-Lan Jones is best remembered as Esmeralda, the hysterical organ-playing Christian recluse who is the first to suggest that Edward Scissorhands isn't the gentle-hearted would-be hairstylist he seems. In **Touch**, her character is such a confirmed ignorant hick that rather than merit the courtesy of a proper name, she's identified by her wardrobe: "Bib Overalls."

Jones's other recurring role is as a food-service professional— "Waitress" in the Bubble Boy episode of **Seinfeld**; "Countergirl" in **Shoot the Moon**; and, in a radical departure, "Viewing Bar Waitress" in **The Truman Show**.

Early in her career, Jones had the potential to go in another direction; she played "Pretty Girl" in **The Right Stuff**. But that was a long time ago. Since then, Jones has staked out her plot of character-actor turf, bringing life to Hollywood's myriad iterations of the slack-jawed redneck. Long may she mouth-breathe.

Edward Scissorhands Esmerelda **1990**		*Mars Attacks!* Sue Ann Norris **1996**		*Clockwatchers* Madame Debbie **1997**
	Natural Born Killers Mabel **1994**		*The End of Violence* Barmaid **1997**	

John Carroll Lynch

HEY! IT'S THAT DOUGHY
GUY WITH HEART!

Stats: **BALD**

AS SEEN ON TV

Balding, doughy guys don't get to fall in love. They don't get the girl, they don't save the day, and they don't clip the bomb's blue wire—not the red one—with two seconds left on the clock.

They do, however, get to be the brother-in-law or the neighbor or the incompetent prison guard or, if they're John Carroll Lynch, the "Impound Manager." When you have a part such as "Impound Manager" on your résumé—as Lynch does, from *Gone in Sixty Seconds*—it's a pretty fair bet that you don't also have "Navy SEAL #3." What you have are parts like "Bartender" or "Prison Guard Walton" or, most famously, Steve, Drew Carey's brother on *The Drew Carey Show*.

Because balding, doughy men don't get to be heroes—unless they, like Lynch, are lucky enough to be in a Coen brothers film. You may remember Lynch as Norm Gunderson in *Fargo*, the stamp-painting husband of Frances McDormand. While he was, at first, a typical balding, doughy guy—in other words, a slow-witted but lovable lug with a taste for junk food and banal pursuits—by the end of the film, he'd emerged as a symbol of solid, trustworthy love in a world of avarice and hate.

Lynch made the most of it, he really did—he shined. And that wasn't just his head.

Volcano Stan Olber **1997**	*Pushing Tin* Dr. Freeze **1999**	*The Good Girl* Jack Field, Your Store Manager **2002**
Face/Off Prison Guard Walton **1997**	*Waking the Dead* Father Mileski **2000**	

HEY! IT'S CHAPTER TWO: THE BACKWOODS

41

Tim Blake Nelson

NEW SCHOOL

TRIPLE THREAT

HEY! IT'S THAT
SUBLITERATE RUBE!

There must be two different Tim Blake Nelsons. One Tim Blake Nelson directs (and often writes) thoughtful, controversial, and daring films—such as *O*, the drama that set *Othello* in a high school, and *The Grey Zone*, a film about Jews pitted against their fellow prisoners in a Nazi prison camp.

Then you've got this other Tim Blake Nelson, who looks like he can't sign his own name, exceptin' for a big black X. He's the flyweight, greasy-haired, ass-scratchin' rube, who shows up in *O Brother, Where Art Thou?* as Delmar O'Donnell, the dingbat country boy. And, why, there he is again in *Minority Report*, as the creepy, organ-tinkling prison warden. And, hey, isn't that him again, as a guy named Bubba, in *The Good Girl*?

Yes, gentle reader, this is one and the same man. Why exactly Nelson—respected actor, daring director, and seasoned writer—is constantly type-cast as a slack-jawed country dunce is a mystery to us.

We like to imagine that he's a real-life idiot savant, discovered in the backwoods and let loose on Hollywood. Maybe he directed *O* in bare feet and overalls with no shirt on and a stalk of buckwheat hanging off his lip, and he was constantly holding up equipment like, say, the boom mike, and proclaiming loudly, "Now, what in dangnation is this thang fawr?"

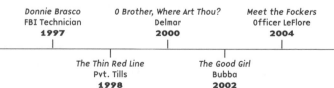

Donnie Brasco	0 Brother, Where Art Thou?	Meet the Fockers
FBI Technician	Delmar	Officer LeFlore
1997	**2000**	**2004**

The Thin Red Line	The Good Girl
Pvt. Tills	Bubba
1998	**2002**

Michael J. Pollard

HEY! IT'S THAT FUNNY-VOICED
MAN-CHILD!

You may know Michael J. Pollard from such roles as C. W. Moss in **Bonnie and Clyde**, or Bug Bailey in **Dick Tracy**, or Mr. Cummings, the slightly lecherous boss, in **Tumbleweeds**. But if you've ever seen Pollard's seminal role as Jahn—the funny-voiced man-child leader of a planet full of renegade, homicidal children in the **Star Trek** episode "Miri," well, then you can never really look at Michael J. Pollard the same way again. In the episode, Captain Kirk and his crew land on a planet curiously devoid of grownups. Suddenly, they are being chased by filthy-faced little urchins, who are led by a strange, funny-voiced man-child named Jahn. Jahn curiously insists on leading these ragamuffins in a chant of "Gr'ups! Gr'ups! Gr'ups!" which makes no sense, until Kirk (and you) figure out that what the little rapscallions are actually saying is a contraction of "Grownups! Grownups! Grownups!"—whom the children loathe. Thanks to this annoyingly infectious phrase, it's very hard to watch Pollard—whether as Andy in **Roxanne** or Owen in **Tango & Cash** or Boner in **I Come in Peace** or in any of the subsequent squirmy, funny-voiced man-child roles that became his bread and butter—without thinking of that infernal chant:

"GR'UPS! GR'UPS! GR'UPS! GR'UPS! GR'UPS! GR'UPS! GR'UPS!"

The Many Loves of Dobie Gillis Jerome Krebs **1959–1963**		*Scrooged* Herman **1988**		*Tumbleweeds* Mr. Cummings **1999**
	Bonnie and Clyde C. W. Moss **1967**		*Dick Tracy* Bug Bailey **1990**	

Michael Rooker

VILLAIN

AWARD NOMINEE

HEY! IT'S THAT MEAN-HEARTED, SQUINTY-EYED SUMBITCH!

No one heads to Hollywood with the idea that they will carve out a career playing mean-hearted, knuckle-dustin', squinty-eyed, racist sons of bitches. But if you are Michael Rooker, and you're squat of build, pug of nose, and squinty of eye, this is exactly the kind of career you carve out.

Here are the highlights: Frank Bailey, the venom-blooded racist thug in *Mississippi Burning*; Chick Gandil, the block-headed, black-hearted first baseman in *Eight Men Out*; Terry, the psychotic, real-killer-after-all in *Sea of Love*; the beady-eyed, icy-hearted Stan "Zeedo" Zedkov in *The Replacement Killers*. And, of course, his brilliant lead performance in *Henry: Portrait of a Serial Killer*.

That's right: a brilliant *lead* performance. After so many character roles, it was Rooker's way of saying, "Hey, I'm a real actor, you know. Just in case you forgot. So think of that the next time you see me charge onscreen as the local Southern sheriff whose badge can't hide the hate in his heart. Or the next time I'm leading some howling, torch-wielding, kill-crazy mob, chasing through the woods after some poor, sweaty black guy, until some uppity and idealistic FBI agent decides that, this time, he just can't stand by and do nothing, and knees me in the nuts."

Days of Thunder Rowdy Burns **1990**	*Bastard Out of Carolina* Uncle Earle **1996**	*Saving Jessica Lynch* Colonel Curry **2003**

JFK Bill Broussard **1991**	*Rosewood* Sheriff Walker **1997**

Tracey Walter

HEY! IT'S THAT
CREEPY WORM!

Take a look around the backwoods. Crickets chirpin', the moon reflected off the swamp, the lonely sound of someone playing a washboard, the satisfied grunts as granpappy climbs onto his cousin. There are plenty of familiar faces here, but none more so than Tracey Walter.

One of the great pleasures of studying Hey! It's That Guy!s in their natural habitats is looking back over their long careers and the various roles they've played. Tracey Walter may well have the best list of character names of any Hey! It's That Guy!—and that's saying something. He has played a man named Mr. Chicken Lickin'. He has played a man named Wee St. Francis. He has played Frog, Roach, Pooch, and Bloodhound Bob. He has played, simply and eloquently, "The Vagrant."

But perhaps his most telling role is that of "Slave Catcher" in **Beloved**. Think about that for a moment. Not just Slave Keeper—Slave Catcher! Could there be a more reprehensible role? And could there be anyone more ideal to play it than Tracey Walter?

Not because he's reprehensible. But he really is the perfect creepy little worm. He's also beloved for his role as Miller in the cult hit **Repo Man**. He's taken a Mr. Chicken Lickin' and he's kept on tickin'. He is the king of the backwoods, and pretty much everywhere else.

	Annie Hall Actor in Rob's TV Show **1977**		*The Silence of the Lambs* Lamar **1991**		*Erin Brockovich* Charles Embry **2000**
		Young Guns II Beever Smith **1990**		*City Slickers* Cookie **1991**	

Don't just stop dead in the middle of the sidewalk, you rube, or you're likely to get run over (or chased into the subway and shoved in front of a train). The big city is no place for greenhorns, so if you can't handle it, you'd better just climb back up on the turnip truck and head out of town. You need to have all your wits about you to navigate the perilous streets full of surly con men, yappy

HEY! IT'S CHAPTER THREE:
THE BIG CITY

yuppies, rich bitches, mysterious merchants, haughty financiers, and vapid socialites pneumatic both of lip and bosom. But don't worry too much if you need to take a break and collect your thoughts; every coffee shop contains at least one salt-of-the-earth waitress who's happy to listen to your story and prop up your flagging spirits. Before she stabs you to death.

Jane Adams

HEY! IT'S THAT
FRAGILE NEUROTIC!

Jane Adams isn't going to put Jennifer Garner out of business. Kicking ass isn't really Jane Adams's thing. Actually, brushing her teeth without crying isn't really Jane Adams's thing. She plays women who aren't equipped to deal with life's everyday setbacks.

Which is weird, because half the time Adams plays professionals and brainiacs. She's played a psychiatrist (in *Mumford*), an obstetrician (in *Father of the Bride II*), and a plastic surgeon (in a recurring role on *Frasier*). She's played a PBS talk-show host in *You've Got Mail*, a university administrator in *Orange County*, and feminist critic and journalist Ruth Hale in *Mrs. Parker and the Vicious Circle*. But she's so soft-spoken and quivery that you have to wonder how she got through college. Or her MCATs. Or kindergarten.

Adams's birdlike figure and naïve fragility suit her perfectly for playing girl-children who are love's unfortunate playthings. She gets screwed over by not one but two grody paramours—Jon Lovitz and Jared Harris—in the ironically titled *Happiness*. On *Frasier*, she hooked up with Niles, a man long in love with another woman—going so far as to marry him just before he figures out what he wants in life.

Jane Adams may not play roles that entail a lot of glory or majesty, but when it comes to playing frail pushovers, she has no peer.

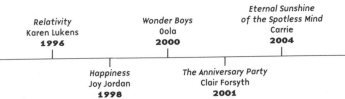

Relativity
Karen Lukens
1996

Wonder Boys
Oola
2000

Eternal Sunshine of the Spotless Mind
Carrie
2004

Happiness
Joy Jordan
1998

The Anniversary Party
Clair Forsyth
2001

Christine Baranski

Stats: **HALL OF FAME**

ICONIC ROLE

AS SEEN ON TV

AWARD WINNER

HEY! IT'S THAT BRITTLE
HIGH-SOCIETY VIXEN!

In 1995, Marcy Carsey and Tom Werner thought it would be a good idea to rip off the popular British series *Absolutely Fabulous*. In the Edina role, they cast the bosomy, hysterical Cybill Shepherd—a poor translation, to make a charitable assessment. But in casting the Patsy role, they improved on the original, beaming the formidable Christine Baranski into American homes every week. *Cybill* was a justly short-lived series, but Baranski's Maryann, a booze-swilling divorcée, was the show's most perversely appealing character.

Baranski has appeared in dozens of movies (including *9½ Weeks*, *Jeffrey*, *Bulworth*, *Bowfinger*, *How the Grinch Stole Christmas*, *Chicago*, and *Marci X*). In addition to the aforementioned *Cybill*, she is also a veteran of the short-lived series *Welcome to New York* and *Happy Family*—two shows that were no doubt greenlit on the strength of her involvement but were far beneath her towering talents.

With her regal bearing, Baranski embodies the screen archetype of the upper-class ice queen—a role she has memorably played in such films as *Reversal of Fortune*, *The Birdcage*, *Welcome to Mooseport*, and two TV-movie adaptations of the beloved *Eloise* children's books. Baranski has staked her claim on the rich bitch, and no one does it better than she.

Reversal of Fortune
Andrea Reynolds
1990

The Ref
Connie Chasseur
1994

Bowfinger
Carol
1999

Addams Family Values
Becky Martin-Granger
1993

Cruel Intentions
Bunny Caldwell
1999

Jennifer Coolidge

HEY! IT'S THAT NYMPHOMANIAC
SOCIALITE!

When it comes to portrayals of the stereotypical rich, white, hot-to-trot matron, Jennifer Coolidge and her apparently pneumatic lips have cornered the market.

Mind you, Jennifer Coolidge didn't always make her living playing nothing but Versace-clad aging bimbos. She first came to our attention on **Seinfeld,** playing Jody, a masseuse who was dating Jerry but refused to massage him and who was doing a poor job of hiding the fact that she disliked George. Swathed in earth tones, wearing a simple, not-at-all-teased hairstyle and virtually no makeup, Jody's look was so sensible, you'd never have guessed that deep inside there was a bleached-blonde skank itching to get out.

Appearing in **American Pie** as Stifler's Mom—a sexed-up caricature of an older woman who seduces one of the friends of her high-school-age son—seems to have tripped some kind of switch in Coolidge; she apparently loved that role so much that she keeps playing it over and over again.

A Night at the Roxbury
Hottie Cop
1998

Best in Show
Sherri Ann Ward Cabot
2000

Legally Blonde
Paulette Bonafonté
2001

American Pie/Pie 2/Wedding
Stifler's Mom
1999/2001/2003

Down to Earth
Mrs. Wellington
2001

In **Best in Show**, she's the sexed-up caricature of a gold-digging trophy wife, with the slight variation that she turns out to be a lesbian who falls in love with her dog trainer. In **Down to Earth**, she's the sexed-up caricature of a gold-digging trophy wife, with the slight variation that she's trying to murder her husband.

In 2004, Coolidge stretched just slightly (okay, really not at all) by playing the rich and nuanced character of Hilary Duff's vapid, over-Botoxed stepmother in **A Cinderella Story** and Joey's vapid, over-collagened agent, Bobbi, on **Joey**. So it's unlikely that she'll close the circle of nymphomaniac socialites and return to playing roles like "Hottie Cop" (from **A Night at the Roxbury**) and "Woman at Football Game" (from **Austin Powers: The Spy Who Shagged Me**) in the foreseeable future. Anyway, there will inevitably be an **American Pie 4** before any of the dudes in its cast can lose too much more hair, so Coolidge has to keep her oversexed rich-bitch muscles toned.

Pootie Tang
Ireenie
2001

A Mighty Wind
Amber Cole
2003

Joey
Bobbi
2004

Legally Blonde 2:
Red, White & Blonde
Paulette Bonafonté
2003

A Cinderella Story
Fiona
2004

HEY! IT'S CHAPTER THREE: THE BIG CITY

51

Frances Fisher

Stats:

HEY! IT'S THAT SMART,
STEELY SPITFIRE!

Every Frances Fisher role is some mix of three predominant attributes: smarts, steeliness, and spitfire-osity. In *Titanic*, Fisher played Ruth DeWitt Bukater, mother to Kate Winslet's Rose. That one was all smarts and steel, as she schemed to shore up the family's declining finances by making Rose a good match. Ruth has no patience for Rose's juvenile romantic notions and points out that marriage is not about love. It's about big, tacky, obscenely expensive jewels. You're damn right, Ruth!

Fisher also plied her particular brand of steel and fire-spitting on NBC's legal drama *The Lyon's Den*. Fisher played Brit Hanley, the smartest and most bad-ass secretary at the firm. Brit was by far the most interesting character on the show—plotting behind the scenes, smashing people's beloved guitars, and slapping her boss right in the kisser! Fisher seemed to be the only one who realized that the show could be a very serviceable pulp drama in the manner of *The Firm* if Rob Lowe didn't insist that his Jack Turner be a morally superior (and therefore dull) hero. Brit ruled.

Here's to you, Frances Fisher. Though it's been dead lo these many moons, we still like to picture you slapping someone on the set of *The Lyon's Den*. Namely, Rob Lowe.

Lucy & Desi: Before the Laughter Lucille Ball **1991**	*The Big Tease* Candy **1999**	*Laws of Attraction* Sara Miller **2004**

Unforgiven Strawberry Alice **1992**	*Blue Car* Delia **2002**

Lee Garlington

**HEY! IT'S THAT
BORED COFFEE-SHOP
WAITRESS!**

In 1989, a sitcom pilot aired on NBC. It had no plot to speak of and little impact on the ratings. But over the next nine years, it became the No. 1 sitcom on TV. It was called *The Seinfeld Chronicles*, later rechristened ***Seinfeld***. This is the story of the woman who played the coffee-shop waitress in the pilot: Lee Garlington.

Garlington has appeared on nearly every long-running TV series you can name, and then some. ***Roseanne***, ***Murphy Brown***, ***Home Improvement***, ***NYPD Blue***, ***L.A. Law***, ***The Practice***. She's played everyone from Joey's father's mistress in the first season of ***Friends*** to Xander's drunken, bitter mother on the penultimate season of ***Buffy the Vampire Slayer***.

Garlington's played cranky schoolteachers (***Some Kind of Wonderful***) and easily shocked mothers (***American Pie 2***). She has also played the bartender, in a '70s-era lesbian bar (***If These Walls Could Talk 2***), and a hugely pregnant Russia expert in the CIA (***The Sum of All Fears***).

Then, in 2002, a movie premiered. An actor well known for playing cuddly characters in family-friendly movies made a major departure, playing an unbalanced, violent man and earning rave reviews. That movie was ***One Hour Photo***, and this has been the story of the woman who plays the coffee-shop waitress: Lee Garlington.

Sneakers Dr. Elena Rhyzkov **1992**	*Friends* Ronni **1995**	*Everwood* Brenda Baxworth **2002**
Jack the Bear Mrs. Festinger **1993**	*Townies* Kathy Donovan **1996**	

Adam Goldberg

HEY! IT'S THAT JITTERY, JEWISH,
GEN-X SIDEKICK!

We can't possibly be the only ones harboring naughty fantasies about being on the receiving end of Adam Goldberg's inimitable glower, just before it breaks into a grin. Can we? Oh, we can? Hey, that's cool. More for us.

Goldberg doesn't exactly display a huge range as an actor: He pretty much always plays a cranky, neurotic, fast-talking, self-deprecating character. His actorly choices consist of ever-so-slightly modulating the levels of crank, neurosis, speed of speech, and self-deprecation. His role as Chandler's new roommate, Eddie, on *Friends*—his first outing as an urban Gen-X sidekick—was, we felt, kind of a rip-off for the viewer. We only had one episode in which we saw him enjoying Chandler's jokes and denigrating *Baywatch* before he turned psycho: watching Chandler while he slept, accusing Chandler of sleeping with his ex-girlfriend, and "forgetting" that Chandler had asked him to move out. It would have been nice to enjoy Eddie's "See ya, pals" a little longer before he became a plot contrivance to keep nonsexual boyfriends Chandler and Joey apart.

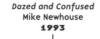

Dazed and Confused
Mike Newhouse
1993

Higher Learning
David Isaacs
1995

Friends
Eddie Menuek
1996

Relativity
Doug
1996–1997

Saving Private Ryan
Pvt. Stanley Mellish
1998

His tent securely pitched on Sidekick Beach, Goldberg moved on to play yet another protagonist's less conventionally attractive urban roommate on *Relativity*, the short-lived ABC drama. Based on this credit, Goldberg still owns the title of Hottest, Gloweringest, Unlikeliest Sex Symbol from a Prematurely Cancelled ABC Drama, despite Jeremy Piven's post-*Cupid* attempts to usurp him.

Though he does the occasional turn as a Jew of Yesteryear (in movies like *Saving Private Ryan* and *A Beautiful Mind*), Goldberg is still at his most Goldbergian playing prickly contemporary urban characters—jerky traders (*The $treet*), jerky lawyers (*Will & Grace*), speed freaks (*The Salton Sea*), and oh, lord, the sidekicks, in forgettable crap like *EdTV* and *How to Lose a Guy in 10 Days*.

These will do until Goldberg gets a chance to play an urban protagonist with a WASPy sidekick. (We know it's not likely, but don't shatter our illusions. Just let us love our Goldberg.)

HEY! IT'S CHAPTER THREE: THE BIG CITY

EdTV		*A Beautiful Mind*		*How to Lose a Guy in 10 Days*
John		Sol		Tony
1999		**2001**		**2003**

	All Over the Guy		*The Hebrew Hammer*	
	Brett		Mordechai Jefferson	
	2001		Carver	

Arye Gross

Stats:

HEY! IT'S THAT HAPLESS, NERDY NEIGHBOR!

AS SEEN ON TV

We doubt Arye Gross is a hapless nerd in real life. In fact, he's a well-regarded actor who's taught at USC and starred in acclaimed stage productions of *Three Sisters*, *Taming of the Shrew*, and *Troilus and Cressida*. But put him onscreen and it's nerd, nerd, nerd, nerd, nerd. And all of them hapless. Completely devoid of hap.

Perhaps you enjoyed Gross's prodigious lack of hap during his stint as Adam Green, one of Ellen DeGeneres's early sidekicks on *Ellen*, a sitcom in which Ellen's apartment served as a kind of hive of haplessness, with Ellen herself as the hap-free queen bee. Or perhaps you reveled in Gross's entirely hap-free performance in *Minority Report*, in which he plays a cuckolded husband who can't even properly stab his wife to death with a pair of scissors before getting chucked sobbing to the carpet by the brawny PreCrime cops.

Gross is, in some sense, haplessness personified—or, at least, the personification of every actor who was ever cast as the guy with the clogged sinuses in the nasal spray commercial. Either way, in a town in which everyone is trying to out-hap everyone else, Gross's complete and unabashed lack of hap is a welcome—and, for him, fortuitous—quality, and we expect great hapless things from him for years to come.

Soul Man Gordon Bloomfeld **1986**	*Ellen* Adam Green **1994–1995**	*Minority Report* Howard Marks **2002**
Tequila Sunrise Andy Leonard **1988**	*Gone in 60 Seconds* James S. Lakewood **2000**	

Philip Seymour Hoffman

Stats: **AWARD NOMINEE**

GRADUATE

HEY! IT'S THAT STARVING ARTIST WHO STILL IS SOMEHOW
KIND OF CHUBBY!

POSSE MEMBER

In the late '90s, Hoffman was among the generation of young, up-and-coming Hey! It's That Guy!s of the new millennium, playing sad losers in movies like *Next Stop Wonderland* and *Happiness*.

But then came 1999: *The Talented Mr. Ripley* (in which he played a spoiled '50s socialite), *Magnolia* (in which he played a kind nurse who was among the film's few genuinely moral touchstones), and *Flawless* (in which he played a drag performer). In the case of *Ripley*, he was—along with Cate Blanchett—embarrassingly better than the material he had to work with. And to eke out an award-worthy performance in a Joel Schumacher movie (as he did in *Flawless*) requires superhuman thespianic talents. In *Magnolia*, his gentle and empathetic nurse helps reunite an estranged father and son and generally holds the entire Partridge family together.

Since then, Hoffman has stayed on his amazing career roll: *Almost Famous. Love Liza. Punch-Drunk Love*.

We can't really call Philip Seymour Hoffman a Hey! It's That Guy! anymore. Philip Seymour Hoffman has graduated, William H. Macy–style, to the realm of celebrity, with all the attendant respect and reverence that entails, but he was so good as a H!ITG! that we can't leave him out.

Twister	The Big Lebowski	Cold Mountain
Dustin Davis	Brandt	Reverend Veasey
1996	**1998**	**2003**

Boogie Nights	State and Main
Scotty J.	Joseph Turner White
1997	**2000**

John C. Reilly

HEY! IT'S THAT LOVABLY
INEPT SCHMUCK!

Up to 2002, John C. Reilly had built a fine career on his uncanny knack for combining, improbably, a lovable ineptitude and a slight air of menace. His credits, until 2002, consisted primarily of mop-topped, "Duh, which way did he go?"–style sidekicks, such as Hatcher in *Casualties of War*, Terry in *The River Wild*, Stevie in *State of Grace*, Pete Connelly in *Hoffa*, or Reed Rothchild in *Boogie Nights*.

But Reilly, with his memorable air of manic cool, always seemed destined to break out of the Hey! It's That Guy! ranks, and in 2002, he did, with style. He appeared in prominent roles in four prominent films: *The Good Girl* (as a doofusy, cuckolded husband), *The Hours* (as a doofusy, not-explicitly-cuckolded husband), *Gangs of New York* (as a fierce brawler) and *Chicago* (as a doofus, most-definitely-cuckolded husband). Some H!ITG!s break out with one huge role (think William H. Macy in *Fargo*) while others,

Days of Thunder
Buck Bretherton
1990

Boogie Nights
Reed Rothchild
1997

Magnolia
Jim Kurring
1999

Casualties of War
PFC Herbert Hatcher
1989

Never Been Kissed
Augustus Strauss
1999

like Reilly, do it with by reaching a critical mass of exposure.

He capped this *annus breakoutilis* by earning a well-deserved Oscar nomination for *Chicago*, and was lauded for all four films. We even saw him being interviewed—all by his lonesome—on *Charlie Rose*, which is pretty much the Hey! It's That Guy! equivalent of a coming-out party. Then he earned the ultimate H!ITG! compliment—an uncredited cameo in Adam Sandler's ***Anger Management***. Nothing says you've made it like an uncredited cameo.

All of which means he's hereby left the ranks of Hey! It's That Guy!-dom, marching proudly up the aisle to receive his graduate's diploma and toss that tassel to, er, whatever side it is you toss it to indicate you've graduated. Because he has.

Here's to you, John C. Reilly. Because the C stands for Congratulations!

The Perfect Storm
Dale "Murph" Murphy
2000

The Hours
Dan Brown
2002

The Aviator
Noah Dietrich
2004

Gangs of New York
"Happy" Jack Mulraney
2002

Anger Management
Arnie Shankman
2003

HEY! IT'S CHAPTER THREE: THE BIG CITY

Isaiah Washington

HEY! IT'S THAT
STREET TOUGH!

VILLAIN

AS SEEN ON TV

Isaiah Washington's played crooks at all points on the criminal food chain, from petty shoplifters to midlevel thugs to the head of an organized criminal enterprise (*Romeo Must Die* and possibly *Hollywood Homicide*—the line between legit businessman and gangsta was pretty blurry).

You probably remember a couple of particularly well-executed scenes of Washington's fictional thugdom:

In *Girl 6* he shoplifts fruit from a bodega—by dropping it into an empty Snugli to which he'd apparently sewn fake baby legs—until the tiny little shopkeeper chases him away, fruit flying everywhere. Funny stuff.

In *Out of Sight*, Jennifer Lopez comes to the house of Washington's character, who starts ineptly coming on to her by telling her all about his dog Tuffy and how Tuffy liked to "tussle." When Washington says that he would give Lopez what "every good bitch wants—a bone," she knocks his ass down with the aid of a telescoping baton and goes, "You wanted to tussle. We tussled," and struts out. That scene was pretty cool.

We've seen quite a few of the movies Washington's made. But generally, we barely remember anything about them. Could be that Washington doesn't make enough of an impression. Or it may just be that he tends to show up in the kind of movies that we rent and then fall asleep in front of.

Strictly Business Hustler **1991**	*Bulworth* Darnell, Nina's Brother **1998**	*Welcome to Collinwood* Leon **2002**

Get on the Bus Kyle **1996**	*True Crime* Frank Louis Beachum **1999**

Victor Wong

HEY! IT'S THAT WIZENED, SLIGHTLY CRAZED, CHINATOWN-DWELLING GURU!

Stats: DECEASED

FOREIGNER

A few deep thoughts on Victor Wong:

1. If you were making a Hollywood movie about Chinese people—like, say, *Year of the Dragon*, or *The Golden Child*, or *The Last Emperor*, or *Shanghai Surprise*, or *The Joy Luck Club*—then you were obligated to include Victor Wong. You could be exempted from this strict rule only if you could prove that nowhere in the script was there call for a wizened, old, slightly crazed, slightly ominous, Chinatown-dwelling, fortune-telling guru. In which case, you were probably not making a Hollywood movie about Chinese people.

2. Did you know that in 1990 there was a film released entitled *Life Is Cheap . . . But Toilet Paper Is Expensive*? Victor Wong does, because he was in it. What part did he play? We don't know. But we're betting it was a wizened, old, slightly crazed, slightly ominous, fortune-telling, Chinatown-dwelling guru. Or maybe a skydiver.

3. Victor Wong passed away on September 12, 2001.

4. Does your résumé include the following roles: Uncle Tam, Harry Yung, Egg Shen, Ho Chong, Birack, Chen Pao Shen, Wah Gey, Ho, Walter Chang, Old Chong, Mr. Wong, and Grandpa Mori? If so, please report to Hey! It's That Guy! heaven, where they are holding a special banquet in your honor, because you are the one and only Victor Wong.

Big Trouble in Little China Egg Shen **1986**	*Tremors* Walter Chang **1990**	*Seven Years in Tibet* Chinese "Amban" **1997**
The Last Emperor Chen Pao Shen **1987**	*The Joy Luck Club* Old Chong, the Piano Teacher **1993**	

Welcome to the courtroom, where our glorious system of justice is put to the test every day. Here you'll find all sorts of legal minds arguing passionately for their clients, whether they're accused murderers, or the People of the State of . . . well, fill in the blank, but come on, it's usually New York. On the side of good are bleeding-heart prosecutors and even bleedier-heartier legal-aid attorneys;

THE COURTROOM

on the side of evil are unscrupulous Mob lawyers and incompetent legacies from the Old Boys' Club. Presiding over it all are judges learned and/or corrupt, hiding all manner of sins under those forgiving (and quite flattering) black robes. Will this court come to order?

Maury Chaykin

HEY! IT'S THAT SOULFUL, SHAMBLING LAWYER!

Maury Chaykin is a man of vast talent; in fact, he's a man of vast everything. He's the patron saint of the hefty pirate, the portly sleuth, the imposing outlaw biker, and the gone-to-pot rock star. It says something about him that at least twice in his career he's played men so large they were housebound: Nero Wolfe on the A&E original series *A Nero Wolfe Mystery* and Desmond Howl, a Brian Wilson-esque rock genius, in the 1994 Canadian film *Whale Music*.

While he hasn't found many roles in which his size wasn't the focus, Chaykin is a talented actor. He probably could have made a career just playing Southern lawyers, fanning himself with a straw hat and explaining that, while he may not know from book-learnin', he does know right from wrong.

But Chaykin's a versatile man, so he's equally adept at playing meek pushovers and vicious crooks. He's played everything from knights to computer nerds. And he's proved an inspiration to shambling men everywhere, a worthy icon who casts a jumbo-sized silhouette.

And, you know, if we had to be housebound with someone, Chaykin would probably be a pretty entertaining guy to have around. Just as long as he didn't show us his bedsores. Because, you know, housebound people sometimes get bedsores.

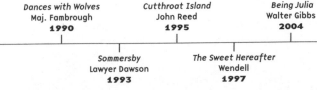

Dances with Wolves
Maj. Fambrough
1990

Sommersby
Lawyer Dawson
1993

Cutthroat Island
John Reed
1995

The Sweet Hereafter
Wendell
1997

Being Julia
Walter Gibbs
2004

Tovah Feldshuh

HEY! IT'S THAT TENACIOUS YET WARMHEARTED LAWYER!

There are roughly four kinds of lawyers who show up in make-believe courts. You've got your rambunctious rebel (often a South'ner), who wears ill-fitting suits and spouts folksy wisdom. You've got your by-the-book D.A. You've got your former-wunderkind-turned-alcoholic washout, who's got to dry out for one last case, because this one means something, dammit.

Lastly, you've got your tenacious, tough-as-nails crusader. That's Tovah Feldshuh—or, at least, her semirecurring character on **Law & Order**, Danielle Melnick. Or, at least, that was her semirecurring character until she turned crooked and got implicated in one of her clients' crimes. But there are still plenty of ways you can get your Feldshuh. She's lent her mix of stern resolve and comforting, mother-hen wisdom to roles in dozens of films, often portraying meddling Jewish women or caring Jewish women or meddling, caring Jewish women. She earned a Tony nomination for her portrayal of onetime Israeli Prime Minister Golda Meir.

We'll go on record as saying, if we're ever wrongfully accused of a crime, we'd love to have her at our side. Though we wouldn't mind the rambunctious rebel either, just because he's always dropping his files, pretending to be a bumbler, which is kind of funny to watch.

Holocaust
Helena Slomova
1978

A Walk on the Moon
Lilian Kantrowitz
1999

Kissing Jessica Stein
Judy Stein
2001

Law & Order
Danielle Melnick
1990

The Corruptor
U.S. Attorney Margaret Wheeler
1999

John Heard

HEY! IT'S THAT PRISSY, IMPOTENT, POTENTIALLY
CORRUPT D.A.!

Hi, I'm John Heard. I'm not John Hurt. I'm also not John Glover. Both of them are craggy, fiftyish British men (okay, fine, Glover's American, but he might as well be British), whereas I'm a tight-assed American with a talent for cinematic bluster. You probably know me best from my role as Tom Hanks's antagonist in **Big**. Indeed, that role does stand as the apex of my career playing bland yuppie scum.

What I bring to all my roles is a subtle mournfulness, because only I know what it is to carry the white man's burden. Once, that burden was a shameful, sexy secret, as when I slept with an attractive young married woman in the seventeenth century and basically ruined her life (in **The Scarlet Letter**). It's not the best position to be in when one is a minister in a small Puritan settlement, but at least there was the frisson of sexual intrigue about it.

The Scarlet Letter
Arthur Dimmesdale
1979

Big
Paul
1988

Home Alone
Peter McCallister
1990

The Seventh Sign
Reverend
1988

Beaches
John Pierce
1988

Home Alone 2:
Lost in New York
Peter McCallister
1992

And now? Mine is the burden of puffy self-satisfaction that's destined to be punctured (if not annihilated) by some man-child or other. It's the burden of having built a life based on all of society's male myths, and then finding myself in a situation that shows me how false all those myths are. It's the burden of portraying interchangeable WASPy patriarchs with ridiculous names like Warren Vandergeld, Willcox Hillyer, and Roone Arledge. It's the burden of watching Elizabeth Perkins date a 30-year-old virgin, in spite of the fact that I play squash and drive a BMW.

I'd like to bust out of my mold. I really would. But look at me. I'm humorless and prim. I'll never be a leading man; I was made to be an obstacle to the leading man's happiness, and that's all I'll ever be.

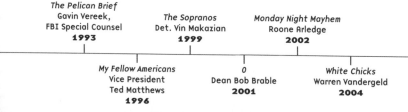

The Pelican Brief
Gavin Vereek,
FBI Special Counsel
1993

My Fellow Americans
Vice President
Ted Matthews
1996

The Sopranos
Det. Vin Makazian
1999

0
Dean Bob Brable
2001

Monday Night Mayhem
Roone Arledge
2002

White Chicks
Warren Vandergeld
2004

Richard Jenkins

HEY! IT'S THAT LAWYER WHO
ISN'T AS UPTIGHT
AS YOU THOUGHT!

Some would say that Richard Jenkins hasn't been a Hey! It's That Guy! since June 2001, when *Six Feet Under* premiered. It's fitting that Nathaniel should be the role for which most of us know Jenkins, since Nathaniel is like Jenkins's whole filmography in microcosm: a fiftyish fellow who comes across as very rigid and uptight but then loosens up and proves that he's been waiting for something to free him—that something being . . . well, death. Sort of. In "The Room," his older son, Nathaniel Jr., finds out about the Late Nate's clandestine pot smoking—and also his modest charity, secretly assisting families unable to pay for funerals.

Nate's hidden reserves of unreserve are gradually revealed, as in all classic Jenkins roles. In *Flirting with Disaster*, Jenkins plays Paul, an ATF agent. Paul is the prototypical bad cop, acting like a total hard-ass to the hapless Mel (Ben Stiller). Through a circuitous turn of events, Paul is served

The Witches of Eastwick
Clyde Alden
1987

And the Band Played On
Dr. Marc Conant
1993

Flirting with Disaster
Paul
1996

Six Feet Under
Nathaniel Fisher Sr.
2001–

a dinner laced with LSD and spends the next several hours running through the desert in his underwear. Once he's started coming down, the formerly strait-laced ATF agent describes the experience, which "continues to evolve" through him.

In smaller roles, Jenkins's characters "loosen up" by having loose morals. In **Changing Lanes**, Jenkins plays a seemingly average law-firm partner who turns out to be basically conscience-free. In **The Man Who Wasn't There**, Jenkins plays a lawyer again—a high-functioning alcoholic who doesn't mind his teenaged daughter spending a lot of time with a much older man. One of Jenkins's latest roles is—surprise!—a lawyer again, this time with Catherine Zeta-Jones in **Intolerable Cruelty**. Working as a divorce lawyer for a raven-tressed man-eater does, of course, require Jenkins to stay as loose as his client's morals.

The Man Who Wasn't There
Walter Abundas
2001

The Core
Gen. Thomas Purcell
2003

Shall We Dance
Devine
2004

Changing Lanes
Walter Arnell
2002

Intolerable Cruelty
Freddy Bender
2003

Ron Leibman

Stats: **AWARD WINNER**

HEY! IT'S THAT PUSHY, UNLIKABLE
DEFENSE ATTORNEY!

VILLAIN

AS SEEN ON TV

MULTI-ETHNIC

Dr. Leonard Green, father to Jennifer Aniston's character Rachel on the sitcom *Friends*, is only one of the many pushy bastards Leibman has played.

Don't confuse Ron Leibman with Ron Rifkin (page 74). They are both sixtyish Jewish actors named Ron, they've both played defense attorneys on *Law & Order*, and they starred together in a 1978 TV movie called *A Question of Guilt*. Also, Leibman played a character named Rivkin. We can see where you might get confused.

Leibman's first pushy bastard was Reuben Warshawky in *Norma Rae*. Reuben is a kind of freelance union organizer who shows up at the factory where Norma Rae (Sally Field) works and raises her consciousness through savvy labor-movement know-how and pure sex appeal. Those of you who are accustomed to seeing him in the present day may be surprised to learn that Leibman was hot in the '70s. The scenes in which he's all disheveled and sweaty and lit from within with the fire of righteousness . . . well, he's tasty enough to turn Liddy Dole socialist.

Sadly, the end of *Friends* has meant the end of Dr. Leonard Green. That schmuck Ross didn't end up on the receiving end of Dr. Green's contemptuously withering glares nearly enough for our taste.

Norma Rae Reuben Warshawky **1979**	*Personal Velocity: Three Portraits* Avram **2002**	*Garden State* Dr. Cohen **2004**

Night Falls on Manhattan Morgenstern **1997**	*Auto Focus* Lenny **2002**

Bruce McGill

Stats: ICONIC ROLE

HEY! IT'S THAT
SLAB-FACED JUDGE!

PERIOD PIECE

It's somewhat ironic that Bruce McGill, who came to the world's attention as Daniel "D-Day" Day, the hard-partying frat brother in **Animal House**, would go on to become such a cinematic emblem of peace, law, and order. Which is exactly what McGill is, when he isn't playing crooks, corrupt cops, baseball managers, blacksmiths, and a guy named Weird Ernie (in the first episode of the early-'90s sci-fi TV series **Quantum Leap**.)

For all that, though, there are very few actors who look better banging a gavel than Bruce McGill. He's got a slab-faced intensity that's just perfect for onscreen judges. Of course, slab-faced intensity also has a timeless feel—as appropriate to a mustachioed barber as to a Prohibition-era copper—which may explain why he often turns up in period films, like **Cinderella Man** or **The Legend of Bagger Vance**.

This raises an interesting question: If John Belushi, the Platonic ideal of hard-partying frat brothers, had lived into his later years, might he have played a judge in a film like **Runaway Jury**? The Republican senator in **Legally Blonde 2: Red, White & Blonde**? No, of course not. Because, frankly, for all his skills, Belushi didn't have Bruce McGill's slab-faced intensity. Though we're sure they could have found a role for Belushi on **Quantum Leap**.

HEY! IT'S CHAPTER FOUR: THE COURTROOM

Silkwood
Mace Hurley
1983

The Legend of Bagger Vance
Walter Hagen
2000

Runaway Jury
Judge Harkin
2003

The Insider
Ron Motley
1999

Legally Blonde 2: Red, White & Blonde
Stanford Marks
2003

71

Austin Pendleton

Stats:

PERIOD PIECE

AS SEEN ON TV

HEY! IT'S THAT DWEEBY JUDGE/
DEFENSE ATTORNEY!

Austin Pendleton has so completely become the personification of querulous cinematic wussiness that he practically doesn't even have to speak to convey it.

Austin Pendleton put himself in our eyeline early in our childhood when he starred in *The Muppet Movie* as Max, Smithers-esque toady to supervillain Doc Hopper. Max is the best role an actor like Pendleton can hope for: wussy but ultimately redeemed by his generosity of spirit toward a band of felt puppets.

Pendleton went on to play many other ineffectual weenies: a stammering defense lawyer in *My Cousin Vinny*, an unhinged ex-chess phenom in *Searching for Bobby Fischer*, a neurotic tropical fish in *Finding Nemo*. But we can also point to a recent instance when Pendleton played a character unlike his usual type. Kind of. In the hundredth episode of *Law & Order: Special Victims Unit*, Pendleton played Horace Gorman, whose special kink was abducting young women and keeping them as sex slaves in an underground dungeon. Even as an extremely perverted sexual predator, Gorman was ineffectual: He not only didn't get away with it, but he ended up with his genitals cut off as the episode began and stabbed to death before it was half over. If they ever make a live-action Ziggy movie, this poor fool should be at the top of the casting director's wish list.

Trial and Error	*Homicide: Life on the Street*	*A Beautiful Mind*
Judge Paul Z. Graff	Dr. George Griscom	Thomas King
1997	**1998–1999**	**2001**

Amistad	*Oz*
Professor Gibbs	William Giles
1997	**1998–2002**

Oliver Platt

HEY! IT'S THAT BLOVIATING
BLOWHARD!

CANADIAN

AWARD NOMINEE

MULTI-ETHNIC

PERIOD PIECE

Even in still photographs, there's something about Oliver Platt's mouth that looks like it's just waiting for its next opportunity to start flapping. His is not a face that's silent very much, and somehow you can tell that just by looking at it.

When Platt was younger and less doughy, his motor-mouthedness suited him to play yuppie upstarts like green yet know-it-all movie producers (**Postcards from the Edge**) and striving architects/sidekicks (**Indecent Proposal**) and sci-fi med students (**Flatliners**).

Platt's talent for being loud and showy landed him roles like Paul Bunyan in **Tall Tale** (no CG required) and, a few years later, a post-hippie Robert Bly type in **Lake Placid**, from which we learned two things: Oliver Platt has worn love beads, and Betty White can curse like a sailor. Both of these things were profoundly disturbing to us.

Platt has also put his gift for gab to work in the fictional legal arena—in Grisham adaptations (**A Time to Kill**) and political dramas (**The West Wing**). Platt was promoted to playing a judge in the short-lived New York Supreme Court TV series **Queens Supreme**. Clueless viewers who tuned in expecting to see CBS's answer to *Queer Eye for the Straight Guy* were disappointed, although who knows what Platt might have been hiding beneath his robe?

Funny Bones
Tommy Fawkes
1995

The West Wing
Oliver Babish
2001

Pieces of April
Jim Burns
2003

Bulworth
Dennis Murphy
1998

Queens Supreme
Judge Jack Moran
2003

Ron Rifkin

MULTI-ETHNIC

BALD

AS SEEN ON TV

VILLAIN

HEY! IT'S THAT TINY, JERKY, ELFIN **ATTORNEY/JUDGE!**

Every time we see Ron Rifkin on-screen, he's playing a complete bastard. Well, not quite: Generally, he plays an outwardly kindly, genial fellow who turns out to be a bastard. Rifkin's twinkly eyes camouflage his nefarious purposes as a crooked D.A. in *L.A. Confidential*. In *Keeping the Faith*, it's not until he starts lecturing Ben Stiller's Rabbi Jake that you realize how intolerant and pissy he is. When he turns up as Giovanni Ribisi's judge father in *Boiler Room*, it's easy to be on his side, because Ribisi's Seth is such a droopy, whiny, criminal, but the movie would have us believe that Seth became the sad sack we see on the screen because he was denied his father's love as a child. In *The Negotiator*, a tale of police corruption, we're not entirely sure who the culprit is; Rifkin fades into the wallpaper amid such Hey! It's That Guy!s as Paul Giamatti (page 144) and J.T. Walsh (page 102), so when he reveals himself as the bad guy, we're left to marvel, "Oh, right. What a bastard!"

Ron Rifkin must exude some kind of ineffable goodness that makes the creeps he plays seem nice—at first. Take Arvin Sloane, his character on *Alias*. Without that sweet veneer to cover his innate depravity, he would have stayed another faceless yet legitimate CIA agent rather than becoming a successful supervillain. God love him.

One Day at a Time Nick Handris **1980–1981**	*Manhattan Murder Mystery* Sy **1993**	*The Sum of All Fears* Secretary of State Sidney Owens **2002**
Husbands and Wives Richard, Rain's Analyst **1992**	*The Substance of Fire* Isaac Geldhart **1996**	

Holland Taylor

Stats: **AWARD WINNER**

AS SEEN ON TV

**HEY! IT'S THAT
SNOOTY JUDGE, AMONG OTHER
BOSSY TYPES!**

No one does icy condescension like Holland Taylor. We aspire to attain her ability to crush a human spirit; she makes it look so effortless.

Our experience of Holland Taylor chiefly involves her roles as middle-aged moms and distaff authority figures. She's mothered Kevin Bacon (in *She's Having a Baby*), Nicole Kidman (in *To Die For*), Michelle Pfeiffer (in *One Fine Day*), Hope Davis (in *Next Stop, Wonderland*), Jim Carrey (in *The Truman Show*), Rena Sofer (in *Keeping the Faith*), and Carla Gugino (in the *Spy Kids* franchise). She's presided over courtrooms (and over Michael Badalucco's Jimmy Berluti) as Judge Roberta Kittleson on *The Practice*. She taught Reese Witherspoon law in *Legally Blonde*. She's played doctors and therapists and a college dean and even Nancy Reagan.

Taylor is also one of the few 59-year-old actresses currently working in TV and film whose characters have libidos—and not libidos that are played for cheap laughs, either. In *Next Stop, Wonderland*, she squires about male models younger than her daughter. Similarly, on *The Practice*, her sex appeal practically enslaves a man more than a decade younger than her. She's totally believable as an AARP-age hottie.

And the contempt she shows Antonio Banderas's little mustache in *Spy Kids 2* does nothing to diminish our favorable estimation of her.

Bosom Buddies Ruth Dunbar **1980**	*Legally Blonde* Professor Stromwell **2001**	*The Wedding Date* Bunny **2005**

The Naked Truth Camilla Dane **1995–1998**	*The Day Reagan Was Shot* Nancy Reagan **2001**

Welcome to the gentlemen's club. This is the habitat of the made man. The wise guy. The good fella. The entire cast of *Goodfellas*, in fact. Yes, you can almost smell the garlic and hear Tony Bennett crooning in the background as that beefy Mob enforcer whales away on that poor guy's kneecaps. Hey, look who it is, over in the corner—it's that guy with the nickname that describes his most prominent physical feature! No, not him, the other guy. The one who's

THE GENTLEMEN'S CLUB

busy talking to that dimwitted fat guy about the best way to serve osso buco. Yes, this is the realm where the American Dream is dissected metaphorically, again and again and again, by large Italian-American men with too much pomade in their hair. It can be rough, but if you work hard and make the right moves, you'll climb to the top. Just look at James Gandolfini, who went from a nameless enforcer in *True Romance* to Tony Soprano. Salud!

James Gandolfini

HEY! IT'S THAT DYSPEPTIC
MOB BOSS!

When you're just starting out, trying to make your bones, Mob-ing is hard. There's a lot of leg work—both in terms of running all over town hijacking cigarette trucks and such, and in terms of breaking the legs of poor saps who can't pay their vig. You don't need to go to the gym, because your daily business gives you enough of a cardio workout: Why else would so many made guys live in their sweatsuits?

Once you've worked your way up the ladder, there's very little hands-on Mob-ing you need to do. At every level of your organization, there are guys kicking money up to you, and all you have to do is sit—behind a desk at your legitimate front, or in your social club—on your ever-widening ass. And before you know it, you have a huge house, more cars than fingers to count them on, and diabetes.

Money for Nothing Billy Coyle **1993**		*Italian Movie* Angelo **1993**		*The Sopranos* Tony Soprano **1999–2006**
	True Romance Virgil **1993**		*Get Shorty* Bear **1995**	

Before he was a multiple award-winner for playing Tony Soprano, Gandolfini was a Hey! It's That Guy!, playing small-time mobsters and enforcers, with names like Angelo and Bear. Post-Tony, he hasn't really tried to stretch very much—still playing Mob enforcers, like a gay hit man in *The Mexican*, a corrupt prison warden in *The Last Castle*, and an embezzling, adulterous department-store owner in *The Man Who Wasn't There*. The news that he'd play the title character in a biopic about Ernest Hemingway is, therefore, especially odd, unless the story reveals Papa's heretofore unknown obsession with cold cuts and ducks.

The Mexican
Winston Baldry
2001

The Last Castle
Col. Winter
2001

The Man Who Wasn't There
David "Big Dave" Brewster
2001

Be Cool
Bear
2005

Michael Imperioli

HEY! IT'S THAT RABBITY,
BROODING HOOD!

Stats:

GRADUATE

AS SEEN ON TV

AWARD WINNER

Some day, the world will be divided into two groups, distinguished by one simple yet crucial difference in perspective: those who most closely associate Michael Imperioli with his role as Christopher Moltisanti on *The Sopranos* and those who'll always think of him as Spider, the put-upon drink fetcher in Martin Scorsese's *Goodfellas*. The latter part launched his career; the former solidified it. And they don't just bookend his résumé; they demonstrate his two divergent strengths.

Christopher is a classic mafia hothead: passionate, brooding, and destructive, yet alluring. Spider was a dipstick who got shot in the foot, then mouthed off to Joe Pesci. And we all know what happens to people who mouth off to Joe Pesci.

In the nine years between *Goodfellas* and *The Sopranos*, Imperioli squeezed in a lot of choice performances, in *Clockers* and *Dead Presidents* and *The Basketball Diaries*, almost all of which fell somewhere on the spectrum from rabbity ne'er-do-well to brooding time bomb. All of these characters, however, have been linked by one mighty attribute: Michael Imperioli's incredible, awe-inspiring eyebrows.

Don't ever pluck, baby.

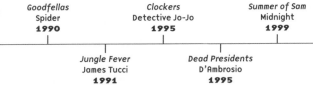

Goodfellas	*Clockers*	*Summer of Sam*
Spider	Detective Jo-Jo	Midnight
1990	**1995**	**1999**

Jungle Fever	*Dead Presidents*
James Tucci	D'Ambrosio
1991	**1995**

Debi Mazar

**HEY! IT'S THAT TRASHY,
POTTY-MOUTHED
MOLL!**

AWARD NOMINEE

VILLAIN

PERIOD PIECE

Debi Mazar characters have exactly the same accent—clipped and flat and surly. She sounds like she'd like to bury her Jimmy Choo so far up your ass that you could taste leather.

Mazar characters are also frequently lower middle class, though always meticulously turned out, with a two-foot wall of hair or a makeup job you can't disturb with a hand grenade.

They're legal secretaries or bank tellers or holders of various other types of stereotypically working-class jobs that are easily performed while wearing extremely long acrylic nails. (Exceptions noted: her subdued *60 Minutes* producer in ***The Insider***, her flinty publicist on ***Entourage***, and her "Young Professional Woman" in ***Collateral***.)

Finally: Debbie De Luca. Ericca Ricce. Sandy Gallo. Denise Ianello. Monica Russo. Mazar characters are Italian. Thick accent, trashy wardrobe, marginal employment, and a surname ending in a vowel. Mafiosa! She's friends with a mobster's ugly gumar (***Goodfellas***) or she's a witness to the Mob (***Witness to the Mob***), and though we never got around to renting such titles as ***Deception***, ***Held for Ransom***, or ***The Deli***, they all sound Mob-y. (The last one's a reach, except that she plays someone named Teresa, and we all know what happens at Satriale's, right?)

Goodfellas Sandy **1990**	*Money for Nothing* Monica Russo **1993**	*That's Life* Jackie O'Grady **2000**
Little Man Tate Gina **1991**	*Trees Lounge* Crystal **1996**	

Alex Rocco

Stats:

ICONIC ROLE

HEY! IT'S THAT
BRAYING BIGMOUTH!

AWARD WINNER

To be honest, Alex Rocco might wonder how he wound up in the Gentlemen's Club. Sure, he's played a few gangsters in his time, but come on—he's no Joe Viterelli or Frank Vincent. He's funny! He was in *Herbie Goes Bananas*!

In order to clear up this confusion, we'd simply stroll up to him and say, "Do you know who you are? You're Moe Greene!"

Greene was the brash, bespectacled, Vegas-based gangster who spat those very words—"Do you know who I am? I'm Moe Greene! I made my bones when you were dating cheerleaders!"—at Michael Corleone in *The Godfather*, much to Greene's regret. (And by "regret," we mean death.)

Rocco went on to varied roles in numerous films, including *Herbie Goes Bananas*, *Cannonball Run 2*, and *That Thing You Do!* And his knack for braying, obnoxious characters has proved effective not only as gangsters but also as salesmen, record-company executives, and, in one instance, a character called the Kumquat Chief.

But to us—and to many people, we suspect—he'll always be Moe Greene, looking up from that massage table, one lens of those trademark spectacles shattered by a bullet, his mouth gaping open as though to issue forth one last braying, ill-considered remark.

	Cannonball Run II Tony **1984**		That Thing You Do! Sol Siler **1996**		The Wedding Planner Salvatore Fiore **2001**
		Get Shorty Jimmy Cap **1995**		Dudley Do-Right Kumquat Chief **1999**	

Frank Sivero

HEY! IT'S THAT WISEGUY
WITH THE ITRO!

PERIOD PIECE

What's an Itro? We're glad you asked. When an African-American person's hairstyle is made up of a lot of short, tight curls in kind of a halo around his head, it's an Afro. When a Jewish person has it, it's a Jewfro. When an Italian person has it, it's an Itro.

Never has a man been so completely defined by his hairstyle as Frank Sivero has been by his. You probably don't remember his character's name in *Goodfellas*, but you remember seeing the back of his head as he hustled his wife, in her illicit fur coat, out of the social club. When *The Simpsons*, in its third season, did a Mob episode with several story elements in common with *Goodfellas*, Fat Tony and his henchmen didn't bear very close resemblance to the characters in the film—all except Louie, who sported the same long, skinny nose and distinctive black Itro as Frankie Carbone.

Sivero—in the same hairdo, eight years later—costarred in *The Wedding Singer* as Adam Sandler's brother-in-law. We don't usually think of films set in the '80s as being period pieces, until you see a 'tro like Sivero's and marvel at how perfectly it sets off his vintage nylon track suit. But then you remember that Sivero is not wearing a period-appropriate wig but his own God-given hair, and you curse the God who could allow such a tonsorial abomination.

The Godfather, Part II		*Goodfellas*		*Little Nicky*
Genco Abbandando		Frankie Carbone		Alumni Hall Announcer
1974		**1990**		**2000**
	Ruthless People		*The Wedding Singer*	
	The Mugger		Andy	
	1986		**1998**	

Mike Starr

Stats:

VILLAIN

AS SEEN ON TV

PERIOD PIECE

HEY! IT'S THAT
BIG LUG!

Mike Starr is always a big lug. Sometimes he gets a name, like Ducky or Frenchy or Vinnie or Fitzie or Mickey or Thumper or Johnny or Tony or, in one memorable case, Pooter-the-Clown. About equally as often, his role is less a character of even two dimensions than a space to be filled with a big lug: "Cell Guard #2" or "Bartender" or "Burglar" or "Doorman" or "Hardhat" or "Bum #3" or the cryptic "Auto Worker Bowling Alley #3."

As *Ed*'s Kenny, Starr wasn't staking out any new territory as an actor; he was a big lug who worked in a bowling alley. However, Kenny is such a big lug because he needs all that room to contain his many layers. Kenny went to Tufts. Kenny had the time of his life singing a duet of "Cruisin'" with an anonymous karaoke/bowling patron. We didn't see much of Kenny, as the producers focused instead on the increasingly tiresome *Moonlighting*-esque travails of Ed and Carol. But Kenny's big lug-ness was almost never played for cheap laughs. It's as if Starr wanted to take the big lug to the next level by imbuing it with so much wit and humanity, and then, having done so, retire his big-lug jersey.

Or maybe not. Case in point: Starr's work as "Block" in *Jersey Girl*.

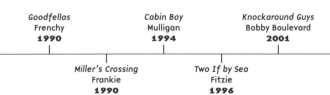

Goodfellas		Cabin Boy		Knockaround Guys
Frenchy		Mulligan		Bobby Boulevard
1990		**1994**		**2001**
	Miller's Crossing		Two If by Sea	
	Frankie		Fitzie	
	1990		**1996**	

Aida Turturro

Stats:

HEY! IT'S THAT BLOWSY, AMORAL
MOB PRINCESS!

When not playing a big-screen waitress of Italian (*Mickey Blue Eyes*), Greek (*Play It to the Bone*), or indeterminate (*Joe Gould's Secret*) ancestry, Turturro portrays Janice Soprano-Baccalieri, sister to James Gandolfini's Tony in HBO's *The Sopranos*. She's been there in so many key moments—stealing a disabled woman's prosthetic leg in a misguided act of revenge; dispatching one fiancé after he dared to strike her; pleasuring another with a sex toy and a lot of grim determination.

In the show's fifth season, Janice finally found herself as a character. Though previous male companions forced her to compromise herself—making love with a gun held to her head, falling asleep at the dinner table after trying to spread "the good news" about Jesus. But in Bobby "Bacala" Baccalieri (Steve Schirripa), Janice has found a mate who accepts her as she is. All he asks of her is that she not mentally abuse his children. Given what we know about her personality, maybe she should find a man who just wants her to straighten her hair.

Aida Turturro has twice played characters named Angie, and she was Geena Davis's costar in the movie *Angie*. If you wanted to draw the conclusion that she is sentenced to her career niche for life without parole, we wouldn't argue very forcefully that you were wrong.

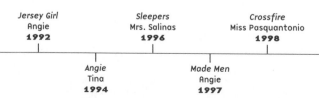

Jersey Girl Angie **1992**		*Sleepers* Mrs. Salinas **1996**		*Crossfire* Miss Pasquantonio **1998**
	Angie Tina **1994**		*Made Men* Angie **1997**	

Frank Vincent

HEY! IT'S THAT GUY YOU
DO NOT WANT TO
MESS WITH!

Stats:

ICONIC ROLE

DOUBLE THREAT

POSSE MEMBER

When Frank Vincent and Joe Pesci first appeared together, in *Raging Bull*, Vincent got lippy, then wound up getting his head smashed in a car door. Then, in *Goodfellas*, while playing his best-known character, Billy Batts, Vincent told Pesci, "Go home and get your shinebox." Not long after, Batts wound up in the trunk of a car, on his way to a hole, and he didn't look so healthy.

You'd think by the time they starred together again in *Casino*, Vincent would have learned to zip his lip. But no. And this time, he gets the last laugh, if by "laugh" you mean "beats Joe Pesci to death and dumps him in a ditch." Which, in the mafia, is what passes for a pretty hilarious practical joke. Gotcha!

Now, for someone who used to be a professional drummer, who played with Del Shannon and Paul Anka, and who bills himself on his Web site as "actor, musician, comedian," Vincent sure is convincing when playing the kind of guy who knows you for twenty years, attends your son's first communion, then one day drives you into the country and, in the middle of a conversation about mascarpone, puts a bullet right behind your ear.

The moral of the story: Frank Vincent can get the best of Joe Pesci, even if it takes three movies. So you don't want to be lipping off to him.

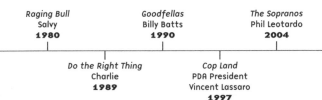

Raging Bull	*Goodfellas*	*The Sopranos*
Salvy	Billy Batts	Phil Leotardo
1980	**1990**	**2004**

Do the Right Thing	*Cop Land*
Charlie	PDA President
1989	Vincent Lassaro
	1997

Joe Viterelli

Stats:

HEY! IT'S THAT FAT, SLOW-WITTED GANGSTER WHO'S KNOWLEDGEABLE ABOUT VEAL!

In every Mob movie, there's always one psycho gangster with an itchy trigger finger. And then there's always one conflicted gangster who has misgivings about the ruthlessness of his profession. And then there's always one big, fat gangster who's kind of slow-witted but really knows a lot about cooking, especially veal.

Joe Viterelli was that last one. The veal-loving gangster.

Near the end of his career—which ended for good in 2004, when Viterelli passed on to the great gentlemen's club in the sky—he'd all but stopped playing actual gangsters and instead was playing goofy gangsters in spoof gangster movies like *Mickey Blue Eyes*, *Analyze This*, and *Jane Austen's Mafia!* But really, everything you need to know about Joe Viterelli is contained in his résumé. Here is a brief sampling of his characters: Fat Charlie, Fat Tony Ragoni, Vinnie "The Shrimp," Dominick Clamato, Salvatore Greco, Mickey, Tony, Didi Giancano, Nick Valenti, Ugolino, Joey Morolto, Gino Marchese, Joe Profaci, Fat Tommy Carducci, Gino.

If you've reached a point in your life at which you've played more than one character named "Fat Blankety-Blank," well, you've probably figured out that 1) you're a man of generous proportions, and 2) you're not renowned far and wide for your ability to "disappear into a role."

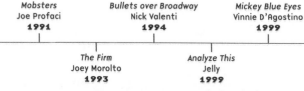

Mobsters
Joe Profaci
1991

The Firm
Joey Morolto
1993

Bullets over Broadway
Nick Valenti
1994

Analyze This
Jelly
1999

Mickey Blue Eyes
Vinnie D'Agostino
1999

Tread carefully in the corridors of power, for you never know what might be waiting around the next corner to permanently alter your existence—and probably not in a good way. Here be, well, not monsters, exactly. But aren't steely, emotionless FBI agents who know seventeen different ways to kill you with a Kleenex at least as scary as any bogeyman? And that's just one kind of governmental operative you don't want to piss off; there are also crooked

HEY! IT'S CHAPTER SIX:
THE GOVERNMENT

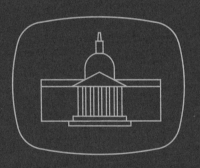

Secret Service agents, sellout senators, amoral chiefs of staff, and even corrupt presidents. Oh sure, there are a few true believers in the *Mr. Smith Goes to Washington* mold, but they're probably just working for positive change in the short term, waiting for their chance to let a big old briefcase full of unmarked bills turn them into wholly owned subsidiaries of Big Tobacco. (Cynical? Who, us?)

Xander Berkeley

Stats: **AWARD NOMINEE**

BALD

HEY! IT'S THAT EVIL, DEAD-EYED CIA/SECRET SERVICE
AGENT!

VILLAIN

Xander Berkeley is shorthand for *evil*. His evil is not always turned up to maximum power, as it was in ***Air Force One***, in which Berkeley plays a dead-eyed Secret Service agent who's secretly working on behalf of airplane-hijacking Russians.

AS SEEN ON TV

Sometimes his evil is only at, like, a 3, quietly humming below the surface, as when he plays Julianne Moore's cold, distant husband in ***Safe***. Sometimes he gets to fan out his campy tail in a display of cartoonish amorality, as he did as a crooked lawman in ***Shanghai Noon*** and as a cowardly, corrupt CIA director on the first two seasons of ***24***.

Our favorite exception to the Berkeley = Evil rule is the 1981 camp classic ***Mommie Dearest***. Berkeley plays the adult version of Joan Crawford's son, Christopher, and is given nothing to do but sport a mop of curly blond hair and try to look shocked as he learns that his deceased mother has left him nothing in her will. Berkeley's appearance is fleeting but gives an impression of things to come; just as Christopher's character is a cipher about whom we learn basically nothing, so will Berkeley come to play average-looking, seemingly neutral characters. Only we'll learn in later movies that his compliant blandness and dead-eyed detachment is a disguise for a core of pure evil.

Terminator 2: Judgment Day	*A Few Good Men*	*Gattaca*
Todd Voight	Capt. Whitaker	Dr. Lamar
1991	**1992**	**1997**

Candyman	*If These Walls Could Talk*
Trevor Lyle	John Barrows
1992	**1996**

James Cromwell

HEY! IT'S THAT BEANPOLE
PRESIDENT!

So imagine you're a hardworking character actor, plugging away in roles like "Priest" in *Oh God, You Devil!* and "Wonder World Motel Desk Clerk" in *Pink Cadillac*. Then one day, your agent sends you a script. The movie's star is a talking pig.

Does this seem like a role with "Oscar nomination" written all over it?

James Cromwell's career must be divided into two phases: Before *Babe* and After *Babe*. Between 1971 and 1995, he had roughly thirty major film and TV credits to his name. In the ten years or so After *Babe*, he piled up more than forty major credits. He's also stepped to the front rank of Hey! It's That Guy!s, playing fictional presidents in cheesy thrillers (*The Sum of All Fears*) and real presidents (*RFK*, playing Lyndon Johnson), as well as cashing in with tiny roles in mega-budget blockbusters. (Cromwell appeared—for about all of thirty seconds—as Dr. Lanning in *I, Robot*.)

Cromwell's proved himself a damn fine actor; for proof, you need only watch his demonic performance in *L.A. Confidential*. He's also proved an able stand-in wherever stern, whippet-thin authoritarians are required. Put him in overalls and hand him a pitchfork: Hello, farmer. Put him in a suit, stand him in front of a flag, and presto: Hail to the chief.

HEY! IT'S CHAPTER SIX: THE GOVERNMENT

Revenge of the Nerds
Mr. Skolnick
1984

The Green Mile
Warden Hal Moores
1999

Angels in America
Henry
2003

Deep Impact
Alan Rittenhouse
1998

Citizen Baines
Elliott Baines
2001

Bruce Davison

AWARD NOMINEE

AS SEEN ON TV

ICONIC ROLE

HEY! IT'S THAT TIGHT-ASSED, INTOLERANT
SENATOR!

What is government but a stern yet loving parent to its citizen-children? It sets rules, it punishes you when you transgress, it rewards you when you do well, and . . . well, *you* have to pay *it* an allowance, which is where the analogy breaks down. But government is, or strives to be, a Decent Dad.

Bruce Davison embodies Decent Dad-ness. He seems to be coiled in a state of coiled readiness, prepared to spring into the middle of the proverbial good fight. Davison's Senator Robert Jefferson Kelly, in the *X-Men* film franchise, acting in loco parentis to his constituents, is concerned that American children not be molested by possibly evil mutants.

Similarly, in ***crazy/beautiful***, Davison's Tom Oakley is a lefty local politician by day and, by night, a beleaguered father unprepared to meet the challenges posed by his daughter's persistent defiance. Davison works hard to dramatize the conflict that is the lifelong condition of both a Decent Dad and a lawmaker. The situation in *crazy/beautiful* may seem exaggerated. After all, your dad has probably never watched you leave with an unsuitable beau, sunk to his knees, reached out after your departing car with one arm and screamed, "NOOOO!" But if you ask, I'll bet he'd say there were times when he wanted to.

Willard
Willard
1971

The Crucible
Reverend Parris
1996

Confession
Father Thomas Parker
2005

Longtime Companion
David
1990

The Practice
Scott Wallace
2000–2001

HEY! IT'S THAT GUY!

Victor Garber

Stats:

HEY! IT'S THAT STRANGELY REFINED CIA **BLACK-OPS AGENT!**

AWARD NOMINEE

GRADUATE

PERIOD PIECE

Jennifer Garner gives the impression that she is the star of **Alias**, because her Sydney Bristow wears the wigs and beats people up; her role in the show is more . . . showy. Her father, Jack, on the other hand—(under)played by Victor Garber—is a veteran of the CIA and an ex-double agent, an expert in game theory, and the smartest person in any room full of smart people. But Jack has secrets! He's owed favors by all kinds of shady people and has access to several warehouses and all manner of spy gear. Jack may not always be on the side of good, but we sense that he sometimes does the wrong thing for the right reason. Or at least a reason that screws over someone in his way. Jack can dispatch a pack of assassins and then have dinner at a four-star restaurant, all without mussing his suit. Bad-ass.

Pre-*Alias*, Garber had less in common with James Bond. Like, Bond seldom breaks into song, whereas Garber is a veteran of musical theater (originating roles in several Stephen Sondheim shows on Broadway) who played no less an icon than Jesus Himself in the film version of **Godspell**.

If only it had been Jack Bristow on the *Titanic* as it sank instead of the ship's designer, Garber's Thomas Andrews. He would have figured out a way to right it and recommended the perfect wine to go with the celebratory dinner.

Liberace: Behind the Music	*Annie*	*Legally Blonde*
Liberace	Daddy Warbucks	Professor Callahan
1988	**1999**	**2001**

Titanic	*Life with Judy Garland:*
Thomas Andrews	*Me and My Shadows*
1997	Michael Sidney "Sid" Luft
	2001

Philip Baker Hall

POSSE MEMBER

ICONIC ROLE

HEY! IT'S THAT CRUSTY, CYNICAL
DEFENSE SECRETARY!

Despite his fin de siècle ubiquity (six films in 1999 and nine in 1998); his favored-actor status with director Paul Thomas Anderson (he appeared in *Magnolia*, *Boogie Nights*, and Anderson's first film, *Hard Eight*); and his consummate Hey! It's That Guy! career (well over seventy movie roles since 1970), we'd wager dollars to donuts that the first thing most people think when they see Philip Baker Hall is, "Hey! It's that guy from *Seinfeld*."

Hall's role in 1990 as library detective Lt. Bookman was to Hall what Hannibal Lecter was to Anthony Hopkins—a signature role late in life that vaults a previously little-known actor into the consciousness of the public. The virtuosic tongue-lashing Hall unleashed on Jerry for his failure to return an overdue book prompted a lengthy ovation from the live studio audience. And the role was classic Hall: world-weary, wizened, and as crusty as dirty undies worn for a third straight day.

We thank *Seinfeld* (with an assist to P. T. Anderson) for opening the Philip Baker Hall floodgates and unleashing this delightful torrent of crust. Though we have to admit that, thanks to Lt. Bookman, it's now hard to watch Hall doing his "let's cut the bullspit" shtick in films like *The Talented Mr. Ripley* without feeling a little bit like giggling.

Say Anything . . . IRS Boss **1989**	*Magnolia* Jimmy Gator **1999**	*The Matador* Mr. Randy **2005**
	Ghostbusters II Police Commissioner **1989**	*The Sum of All Fears* Defense Secretary David Becker **2002**

Lucinda Jenney

Stats:

HEY! IT'S THAT MOUSY, PASSIVE-AGGRESSIVE CONGRESSWOMAN/ POLITICAL WIFE!

Lucinda Jenney is adept at standing in the background of beautifully decorated settings, pressing her lips together, and glowering passive-aggressively at some important rich husband. For instance, Jenney played an upper-class political wife in *crazy/beautiful*. The director probably intended Jenney's character to be an evil stepmother to erratic teenager Kirsten Dunst, but Dunst plays such a shrill, annoying brat that those of us in the audience past high-school age wish we could take Jenney out for lunch and a manicure just to give her a break from her irritating stepdaughter.

Our favorite Jenney performance ever is in *Thelma & Louise*. As "Lena, the waitress," Jenney waits on Susan Sarandon and Geena Davis at the boot-scootin' bar where they stop for a drink. Jenney is friendly but not intrusive, sort of world-weary in that way that lifelong waitresses can sometimes be, and observant enough to recognize a kindred spirit in Sarandon: She accurately pegs Sarandon as a fellow waitress when questioned by police, based on the generosity of Sarandon's tip. In only a few lines of dialogue, Jenney creates a fully rounded character. It's the ability to put on screen that kind of character-in-microcosm that sets the Hey! It's That Guy!s apart from the herd of Hollywood bit players—and why we'll always like Lucinda Jenney. Yes, even in spite of *What Dreams May Come*.

Peggy Sue Got Married Rosalie Testa **1986**		*G.I. Jane* Lt. Blondell **1997**		*S.W.A.T.* Kathy **2003**
	Grace of My Heart Marion **1996**		*The Shield* Lanie Kellis **2003**	

Donald Moffat

Stats: **PERIOD PIECE**

HEY! IT'S THAT BUSHY-BROWED PRESIDENT!

AS SEEN ON TV

In honor of Donald Moffat's 1997 appearance as Walt Whitman on *Dr. Quinn, Medicine Woman*, we offer this Whitman-esque ode to Moffat:

O Donald Moffat!

Tall of stature, gentle of countenance, bushy of brow,

Player of doctors, judges, presidents,

Of generals, colonels, and Garry, that shifty scientist in *The Thing*.

O Donald Moffat! Who looks quite a bit like Lloyd Bridges,

Who is English, yet hides his accent so well,

Who brought his bushy white eyebrows to the film *61**,

in service of the role of Ford Frick.

O Ford Frick! O Moffat! *Is There Life out There?*

This is not a question, but a TV movie you starred in,

As Grandpa Walter.

O Donald Moffat!

Who played President Bennett in *Clear and Present Danger*,

You are a clear and present talent,

O Donald Moffat! Who played Lyndon Johnson in *The Right Stuff*,

You, like those spacemen, like the song by the New Kids on the Block,

Have the right stuff.

The Unbearable Lightness of Being
Chief Surgeon
1988

Regarding Henry
Charlie Cameron
1991

Cookie's Fortune
Jack Palmer
1999

The Bonfire of the Vanities
Mr. McCoy
1990

Tales of the City
Edgar Warfield Halcyon
1993

Will Patton

Stats:

AWARD NOMINEE

BALD

VILLAIN

PERIOD PIECE

HEY! IT'S THAT RUDDY, INTENSE GOVERNMENT **OPERATIVE!**

Hello, I'm Will Patton. My intense, staring eyes, facility with accents, and anonymous cauliflower face have resulted in my being cast as a criminal equally as often as I'm cast as a cop.

Am I chasing down my reckless wife with murder in my eyes (as I did in **The Spitfire Grill**)? Am I gazing at an asteroid on a collision course with the earth (in **Armageddon**)? Am I keeping my nubile daughters away from those boys from the wrong side of the tracks (**Inventing the Abbotts**—it's okay if you can't quite remember that one)? Am I grimly tracking terrorists on a CIA show no one cares about, including me, my wife, and my mom (**The Agency**)? I am all of these things, and more.

There was a time when I thought I might bust out of the character-actor ghetto. It was around the time I was cast as Bethlehem, a supervillain in a movie based on a popular epic science-fiction novel. Unfortunately, that movie turned out to be **The Postman**, an ill-conceived Kevin Costner vanity project, and of the fourteen people who saw it, not one remembered my name. I guess I'll have to wait until TNT does another quickie Civil War movie and needs me to play a Confederate colonel. Screw Kris Kristofferson! It's not like Confederate colonels really need to know how to play guitar; they just need to know how to grow beards. And that I can do.

HEY! IT'S CHAPTER SIX: THE GOVERNMENT

97

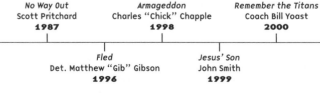

No Way Out	*Armageddon*	*Remember the Titans*
Scott Pritchard	Charles "Chick" Chapple	Coach Bill Yoast
1987	**1998**	**2000**

Fled	*Jesus' Son*
Det. Matthew "Gib" Gibson	John Smith
1996	**1999**

James Rebhorn

Stats: BALD

HEY! IT'S THAT
MENACING, TWO-FACED
AUTHORITY FIGURE!

James Rebhorn probably gets confused with James Cromwell (page 91) quite a bit. Both are tall, both are thin, both are stern, both are named James. Both could, in a pinch, be used as scarecrows. But you know which one would scare the crows more? Rebhorn, that's who.

Cromwell can do menacing, but Rebhorn *is* menacing. Cromwell can be stern, but Rebhorn can be sadistic. Rebhorn looks like the personification of some ominous 1950s dad: stiff, unyielding, and possibly hiding a dark and creepy secret. In short, he's all about the tough love, except without the love.

Take his hardhearted mogul, Herbert Greenleaf, in *The Talented Mr. Ripley*. Or Dr. Larry Banks, who gets trotted out in *Meet the Parents* to further frighten poor Greg Focker. Or his slippery, stubborn defense secretary, Albert Nimziki, in *Independence Day*. Or his menacing salesman in *The Game*. Take them all, please. They're scaring us.

The basic difference between Cromwell and Rebhorn is that you could actually imagine Cromwell giving you a hug. Rebhorn, on the other hand, might hug you, but only to hold you steady before the doctor sticks you with a syringe full of sedative, because they're going to take you to the institution now, which he's decided is for the best.

Basic Instinct	The Game	Cold Mountain
Dr. McElwaine	Jim Feingold	Doctor
1992	**1997**	**2003**

Carlito's Way	Far from Heaven
D.A. Norwalk	Dr. Bowman
1993	**2002**

Saul Rubinek

Stats: PERIOD PIECE

CANADIAN

HEY, IT'S THAT
SWEATY NEBBISH!

Saul Rubinek has spent the past twenty years playing nerds, nebbishes, losers, cowards, yes-men, and Henry Kissinger. Actually, he only played Kissinger once, in 1999's **Dick**. He also starred in **Nixon**, as Herb Klein. But you most likely recognize him as W. W. Beauchamp, the sweaty, lily-livered biographer in Clint Eastwood's **Unforgiven**.

Sadly, his opportunities to play characters named Beauchamp have been limited. In fact, a list of typical Rubinekian parts reads like a roll call at the neighborhood shvitz: Ira Stone, Saul Panzer, Alan Mesnick, Sam Smotherman, Seymour Heller, Hersh Rasseyner, Alan Mintz, and the triumphantly named Eric Schlockmeister.

He also starred in a little-known 1981 Canadian film titled **Ticket to Heaven**, as the wisecracking Jewish best friend of a guy who gets sucked into a Moonie-like cult. The cultists in the film shout "Bomb with love! Bomb with love!" over and over again, a phrase that still gives us the chills. This is because we were shown this film several times at an impressionable age by well-intentioned people who did not, apparently, see the irony in repeatedly showing a film about cults to a bunch of impressionable kids.

Wall Street	True Romance	Rush Hour 2
Harold Salt	Lee Donowitz	Red Dragon Box Man
1987	**1993**	**2001**

The Bonfire of the Vanities	The Family Man	Santa's Slay
Jed Kramer	Alan Mintz	Mr. Green
1990	**2000**	**2005**

Fred Thompson

HEY! IT'S THAT JOWLY
NO-NONSENSE SENATOR!

Fred Thompson, the Hollywood-character-actor slash onetime-U.S.-senator-from-Tennessee, does not exist on what we know of as Earth. No, he exists in some purgatorial astral plane between the corporeal world—or "real life"—and the strange phantom zone that is "celebrity." Why? Let's examine the evidence:

People's Exhibit A: In 1967, Fred Thompson graduates from Vanderbilt law school. In 1973 and 1974, Fred Thompson serves as a Minority Counsel to the Senate Watergate Committee. For real.

People's Exhibit B: In 1977, Thompson helps expose a scandal in Tennessee that leads to the toppling of the governor. The scandal becomes the subject of a best-selling book and, later, a 1985 film called *Marie*, in which Fred Thompson plays himself.

People's Exhibit C: Fred Thompson parlays that role, in which he played himself, into a part on *Matlock*, and then, later, into a successful, Hey! It's That Guy! career, using his hound-dog jowls and no-nonsense Southern drawl to great effect in such thrillers as *No Way Out*, *Fat Man and Little Boy*, *The Hunt for Red October*, *Die Hard 2*, *Class Action*, *Thunderheart*,

No Way Out	*Days of Thunder*	*Class Action*
CIA Director Marshall	Big John	George Getchell
1987	**1990**	**1991**

The Hunt for Red October	*Die Hard 2*
Rear Adm. Joshua Painter	Trudeau
1990	**1990**

and **In the Line of Fire**. He almost invariably plays a lawyer, senator, federal marshal, head of the CIA, or other such muckety-muck.

People's Exhibit D: In 1991, archival footage of the young Fred Thompson testifying at Watergate is included in Oliver Stone's **JFK**.

People's Exhibit E: In 1994, Fred Thompson is elected to the United States Senate.

People's Exhibit F: In 2002, Thompson leaves the Senate to once again become an actor, playing the role of D.A. Arthur Branch on **Law & Order**. In 2004, he introduces George W. Bush at the Republican National Convention in New York.

All of which causes one to wonder: Was Fred Thompson an actual U.S. senator, or did he just play one on TV? Or both? Is Fred Thompson even real?

Sure, there may be Hey! It's That Guy!s more recognizable than Fred Thompson, more successful than Fred Thompson, even more essentially Hey! It's That Guy!-ish than Fred Thompson. But he's definitely the single most important Hey! It's That Personification of the Continued Blurring Between Reality and Our Mediated Experience of Same! Or, at least, the jowliest.

Thunderheart
William Dawes
1993

In the Line of Fire
White House Chief of Staff
Harry Sargent
1993

Law & Order/Trial by Jury
D.A. Arthur Branch
2002–

Born Yesterday
Senator Hedges
1993

Baby's Day Out
FBI Agent Dale Grissom
1994

J. T. Walsh

**HEY! IT'S THAT BLATANTLY EVIL
SENATOR/WHITE HOUSE
ADVISOR!**

VILLAIN

HALL OF FAME

J. T. Walsh was apparently a nice guy. He was president of the
progressive antiwar group Students for a Democratic Society
at the University of Rhode Island. Before becoming an actor,
he was a social worker.

DECEASED

But on-screen . . . total bastard. We're sorry that he's dead
primarily because when Richard Clarke's White House memoir **Against All
Enemies** is turned into a movie, Walsh won't play Dick Cheney. That is how
evil his characters were: amoral, scheming, and generally just plain mean.
And Walsh characters never looked as if doing their various forms of evil
made them happy. From bitter, corrupt army guys (**A Few Good Men**; **Good
Morning, Vietnam**) to dirty cops (**The Negotiator**) to crooked politicians
(**Nixon**), the characters all had the same flat affect and cold, dead eyes. We
can only remember him laughing on-screen once—mirthlessly, as a lawyer
in **The Last Seduction**. And that was as he assisted a felonious client in her
criminal activities and called her a bitch.

We think that, although he is deceased, J. T. Walsh isn't resting in peace.
He's probably reeeeally pissed off. The man spent virtually his entire
professional life being pissed off—and what could possibly piss him off
more than death? It's undignified! It's beneath him.

| Power Jerome Cade, Ohio Senatorial Candidate **1986** | Backdraft Alderman Marty Swayzak **1991** | Sling Blade Charles Bushman **1996** |

| House of Games The Businessman **1987** | Executive Decision Sen. Mavros **1996** |

Harris Yulin

Stats:

AWARD NOMINEE

BALD

PERIOD PIECE

VILLAIN

HEY! IT'S THAT UNETHICAL
CHIEF OF STAFF!

You wouldn't think to be afraid of a sad-eyed old man like Harris Yulin, rapidly pushing 70. You most certainly wouldn't be afraid to encounter him in a dark alley—and about that, at least, you'd be right. Yulin would never lurk in so common a place as a dark alley, waiting to strike, because he doesn't have to: Yulin would strike you in broad daylight, in the middle of a well-lit room, in front of witnesses. And he's such a bad-ass that he'd get away with it, too.

Yulin's characters are quintessentially weary of this world, worn out by its ugliness and many disappointments. No one knows better than those characters all the ways in which humanity and its various institutions can be corrupted and destroyed—primarily because Yulin's characters have been tasked with destroying them.

Yulin's a great villain because his characters generally function on some plane where morality is irrelevant. Characters like crooked White House advisor Roger Stanton (*24*), crappy, absentee father Senator Bell (*The Emperors' Club*), credit-stealing research scientist Edward Manning (*Law & Order*), or cruelly doctrinaire Watchers' Council head (*Buffy the Vampire Slayer*) are so amoral that there isn't even any smug chortling over cognac and cigars—just solitary, joyless bad-itude.

Clear and Present Danger National Security Advisor James Cutter **1994**	*The Hurricane* Leon Friedman **1999**	*24* Roger Stanton **2002–2003**
	Buffy the Vampire Slayer Quentin Travers **1999, 2001, 2002**	*Training Day* Det. Lt. Doug Rosselli **2001**

If you're planning to assemble an international team of ethnically diverse criminals—and, seriously, if you're planning a big job like taking over a skyscraper or hijacking *Air Force One*, you really should think about bringing along a ninja—then this is your one-stop shopping destination. We've got an Asian guy who's good with throwing stars. We've got a seriously mean Latino covered in

HEY! IT'S CHAPTER SEVEN:
THE HIDEOUT

tattoos. We've got vaguely Slavic bad-asses, left over from the Cold War and now available two-for-one, for a limited time! These henchmen offer high-level villainy and ask only one thing in return: that you not dress them in matching costumes and give them all goofy nicknames. Because these are real people with feelings, not a bunch of flying monkeys. Come on.

Erick Avari

HEY! IT'S THAT MYSTERIOUS MAN FROM THE MYSTIC FAR EAST, OR POSSIBLY GREECE!

FOREIGNER

Erick Avari had all of two minutes of screen time in 2003's **Daredevil**, in which he played Elektra's dad, Ambassador Nikolas Natchios (which sounds a bit like an appetizer at TGIFridays). He spent most of his time sweating nervously about the unkind end that we all knew he was destined to meet so that Elektra could be sad, and then mad, and then star in her own sequel.

Avari's two minutes, though, were enough time for a watchful viewer to think, "Hey, isn't that . . . ?" and insert the "Mystic Middle Easterner" role of their choice. Dr. Terrence Bey from **The Mummy**? Kasuf from **Stargate**? Raji from **Encino Man**? Caravan Leader from **The 13th Warrior**?

Avari is, of course, all of those people. Yet he is so much more. He is a respected stage actor. He once starred in **The King and I** on Broadway. He studied under the masterful Indian director Satyajit Ray.

Yet Erick Avari is usually wasted on film. And we don't mean that in the sense of "Cameron Diaz was wasted at the MTV Movie Awards." We mean he was frittered away. Taken for granted. Relegated to a role in which he's upstaged by a camel. Heck, we could have played the part of Ambassador Nikolas Natchios, and we can't even say "Ambassador Nikolas Natchios." Well, not three times fast, anyway.

Stargate Kasuf **1994**	Planet of the Apes Tival **2001**	Daredevil Ambassador Nikolas Natchios **2003**
Independence Day SETI Chief **1996**	Mr. Deeds Cecil Anderson, Blake Media General Counsel **2002**	

Sean Bean

HEY! IT'S THAT MENACING, POSSIBLY IRISH, ROGUE!

Stats:

VILLAIN

MULTI-ETHNIC

WIG/PROSTHESIS USE

Why does Sean Bean look so familiar? Sure, every Hey! It's That Guy! looks familiar, by definition. But Sean Bean seems like he's been in more movies than he's actually been in. And he always seems to be squinting.

Lord of the Rings fanatics will know him primarily as Boromir, the tragically slain human who . . . well, we don't need to explain it: They're fanatics, after all. (As for the rest of us: Boromir, Faramir, who really cares? Just bring on the Orcs!)

For non-*LOTR* devotees, Bean will be familiar as the squinting, possibly Irish, guy who projects an air of menace. Which is ironic, since he's not actually Irish, but was born in Sheffield, England. He's played his share of heavies, though, in films from *Goldeneye* and *Ronin* to *Patriot Games* and *Don't Say a Word*.

This is not a slight, but a testament to Bean's menacing roguishness. He is, in fact, so intrinsically a menacing rogue that, when we once read an interview with him in which he talked about how nice it was, in *Lord of the Rings*, to finally play a hero and not a menacing rogue, we paused, because we were pretty sure he *did* play a menacing rogue in *Lord of the Rings*.

Patriot Games Sean Miller **1992**		*Ronin* Spence **1998**		*Troy* Odysseus **2004**
	Goldeneye Alex Trevelyan **1995**		*Don't Say a Word* Patrick Koster **2001**	

Steve Buscemi

HEY! IT'S THAT SQUIRRELLY
MOTORMOUTH!

For most of his career, Steve Buscemi has been Hollywood's go-to skinny weirdo. It's taken some time for us all to notice that Buscemi is more than just a non-pretty face; he's a pretty bad-ass actor, too. Certainly, he's taken plenty of character roles that didn't tax his skills. But it's not like he did nothing but yappy wiseguy roles until **Fargo**. Sensitive gay man living with AIDS? Gentle bowler? Tough-love-dispensing addiction counselor? Drawling southern poet? Buscemi's done it all. Steve Buscemi: Chameleon.

Buscemi is also a fine director. He collected his indie buddies for **Trees Lounge** a few years back. He directed a couple of **Sopranos** episodes before getting invited back as a cast member in the show's fifth season. Steve Buscemi: Renaissance Man.

But no matter what else Steve Buscemi ever is, he's always "kinda funny-lookin'," which means he's probably doomed to stay in the Hey! It's That Guy! ghetto forever—liver lips never won fair lady, etc. Or so we

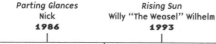

Parting Glances
Nick
1986

Reservoir Dogs
Mr. Pink
1992

Rising Sun
Willy "The Weasel" Wilhelm
1993

Ed and His Dead Mother
Ed Chilton
1993

Living in Oblivion
Nick Reve
1995

thought, until *Ghost World*. It's an unconventional love story, but Buscemi manages to make Seymour, the object of Enid's fleeting affection, much more than an amusingly eccentric curiosity. By the time a drunken Enid seduces him, we can see in Seymour what Enid does, and their hookup seems weirdly right. Steve Buscemi: Lady-Killer!

Unfortunately, we are not exactly overrun with unconventional love stories in which Buscemi could star. Even when he did a Sandra Bullock joint, he was playing pretty much the only man in the film who could not be her love interest (her therapist). And it's a shame, because the hypothetical movies in which Steve Buscemi could play the, yes, fine, funny-lookin' romantic lead are the kind of movie we'd like to see. And we'd take Buscemi's face, full of character—bug eyes, liver lips, and all— over a posse of bland Paul Walker pretty-boys any day of the week. Steve Buscemi: Our Hero.

Billy Madison
Danny McGrath
1995

The Big Lebowski
Donny
1998

The Sopranos
Tony Blundetto
2004

Fargo
Carl Showalter
1996

Monsters, Inc.
Randall
2001

Clifton Collins Jr.

Stats:

AWARD WINNER

MULTI-ETHNIC

VILLAIN

AS SEEN ON TV

HEY! IT'S THAT EASILY BROKEN
FANCY-PANTS!

If being big and tough were a prerequisite for membership in a criminal enterprise, there would be no need for guns. That, however, is not the way it is in Hollywood: While gangs tend to keep around a few big hurly dudes, no crew is complete without some skinny, whiny little sissy. You know, the guy who only got onto the crew because of his tougher grandfather or uncle. Kids get spoiled growing up with inherited wealth, whether their forebears were robber barons or just regular robbers. So crooks' spawn, like all fictional rich brats, end up lazy, soft, ineffective, and decadent, easily taken in by such stings as a condom on a cigarette pack in a seedy gay bar. Yes, Frankie Flowers, we're talking about you.

Clifton Collins Jr.'s performance in *Traffic*, as Francisco "Frankie Flowers" Flores, probably didn't put him in the running for any GLAAD awards, and not just because of the poor, wispy quality of his bad teenage mustache. Frankie's attraction to men is the very means the cops use to get his attention. Maybe they release him back into the population after his torture in a Mexican prison because they think they've broken him—but here's where Frankie really does his people (both criminals and gays) proud: He accepts an assassination job, and gets right back on the horse.

| *One Eight Seven* Cesar Sanchez **1997** | *The Rules of Attraction* Rupert Guest **2002** | *The Hillside Strangler* Kenneth Bianchi **2004** |

| *The Last Castle* Cpl. Ramon Aguilar **2001** | *Undefeated* Loco **2003** |

Robert Davi

HEY! IT'S THAT
UNSCRUPULOUS, SNEERING
DRUG LORD!

Stats: MULTI-ETHNIC

STRAIGHT-TO-VIDEO

We imagine that, for someone who specializes in screen villains, getting to play a Bond bad guy would be the high point of your career—something after which you could die happy.

We also imagine that starring in straight-to-video pot-boilers like *Soulkeeper*, *Absolute Aggression*, *Codename: Silencer* and *Maniac 3: Badge of Silence* would not represent the high point of your career— rather, they'd be films after which you could easily die of embarrassment.

Either way, the best person to ask is Robert Davi. Davi, who looks a bit like the love child of James Woods and Rob Lowe, is best known to most of us as the arrogant FBI agent in *Die Hard*, the cop in *Predator 2*, or, of course, the greasy drug lord in the actually pretty terrible 1989 Bond film *License to Kill*. (Let's just say that Davi's character, Franz Sanchez, didn't exactly get enshrined along with Oddjob and Blofeld in Bond's All-Star Hall of Infamy.) To some of us, though, he's best known for his work in movies with words like *maximum* or *justice* or *behavior* or *dangerous* in the title. (*Maximum Justice! Dangerous Behavior! Absolute Maximum!*—try it, it's fun!) Which is to say, the rest of us need to get out more often.

Raw Deal	*Die Hard*	*The Hot Chick*
Max Keller	FBI Special Agent Johnson	Stan Thomas
1986	**1988**	**2002**

Action Jackson	*Showgirls*	*The Film Maker*
Tony Moretti	Al Torres	Rodriguez
1988	**1995**	**2005**

Billy Drago

**HEY! IT'S THAT
WEASELLY, PINCH-FACED
BASTARD!**

There was a time (we'll call it "the early '80s"), when Billy Drago, né Billy Eugene Burrows, had staked out quite a nice little niche for himself as a squinty-eyed bad-ass. He employed said squinty eyes and said bad ass in various roles as renegade commandos, crooked lawmen, and, most famously, as the weaselly pinch-faced bastard and gangland assassin, Frank Nitti, in 1987's *The Untouchables*—you know, the guy who meets his end by getting chucked from a rooftop and crashing into a Model T Ford.

Since then, Mr. Drago has disappeared into the netherworld of straight-to-video releases, and you probably haven't seen him unless you're prone to renting films such as *Death Ring*, *Sci-Fighters*, *Blood Money*, or *Convict 762*. We're not sure why Drago's career took this turn. Perhaps it was due to some confusion between himself and Drago, the Soviet pugilist in *Rocky IV*. Perhaps at the dawn of the sensitive '90s—that was, after all, the time of *Regarding Henry*—the demand for weaselly

Pale Rider
Deputy Mather
1985

Vamp
Snow
1986

The Untouchables
Frank Nitti
1987

Delta Force 2:
Operation Stranglehold
Ramon Cota
1990

Guncrazy
Hank Fulton
1992

pinch-faced bastards in mainstream films dwindled away. Or perhaps Mr. Drago simply chose to take refuge in the comforting world of the video store's bottom shelf, where he can make a tidy living playing characters named Mannix and Reverend James and Billy "Spider" Masters. We like to think it's the latter.

In any case, we feel it's only right to reserve the last word not for us, but for a Brazilian fan of Billy Drago's who hosts a Web site called "Jackie's Billy Drago Page":

"Incredible, his power of enthralling us. Billy has an aura that shines even when the scene requires he remains immovable. . . . For those who have not seen him yet, I recommend them to consult his filmography and find out the acting show that awaits for them!"

We're with you, Jackie. We're with you.

Death Ring
Danton Vachs
1993

Charmed
Demon of Fear/Barbas
1999–2004

Nash Bridges
Lou Grissom
1999

Tremors 4: The Legend Begins
Black Hand Kelly
2004

William Fichtner

Stats: VILLAIN

HEY! IT'S THAT
JUMPY, INTENSE, STRANGELY
HANDSOME HOODLUM!

William Fichtner is so close. Close to what? To graduating from Hey! It's That Guy! status and joining the ranks of ex–Hey! It's That Guy!s such as William H. Macy, Phillip Seymour Hoffman (page 57), and John C. Reilly (page 58) in their post–Hey! It's That Guy! glory. Like them, Fichtner has patiently served his celebrity apprenticeship. Now he stands poised to step into the relatively blinding sort-of spotlight that is minor celebrity.

Fichtner didn't make this leap after *Passion of Mind*, a dismal flop best remembered as the film after which America finally, totally decided they never wanted to see Demi Moore again. Nor did it happen after *The Perfect Storm*, a water-logged dud.

And so, we continue to wait. Which isn't so bad, because in the meantime, we get to enjoy the jumpy energy and steely intensity that's served Fichtner so well in all his movies up to now: the movies in which he's played uptight army men or on-the-edge cops or barely-reined-in thugs. You know, like his twisted drug-enforcement agent in *Go* or his tight-assed colonel in *Armageddon* or his blind doctor in *Contact* or his twitchy wingman in *Heat* or his hair-trigger psycho in *Albino Alligator*.

But trust us: It's only a matter of time. We're not predicting Tom Cruise–style celebrity; more like Ed Harris–style celebrity.

	Armageddon	
Strange Days	Col. William Sharp,	*Black Hawk Down*
Dwayne Engelman	Shuttle Freedom Pilot	SFC Jeff Sanderson
1995	**1998**	**2001**

Contact	*The Perfect Storm*
Kent Clark	David "Sully" Sullivan
1997	**2000**

Brendan Gleeson

MULTI-ETHNIC

FOREIGNER

WIG/PROSTHESIS USE

PERIOD PIECE

HEY! IT'S THAT TOUCHINGLY AFFABLE AND/OR MURDEROUS IRISHMAN!

Brendan Gleeson has played plenty of paternal Irishmen over the years, in such shamrock-infested films as *Far and Away* and *Michael Collins*. For us, he's had the most impact in *Gangs of New York* and *28 Days Later . . .*

In *Gangs*, Gleeson is both affable and murderous as Monk. Monk's talent is bashing people's heads in with a bloody club. But Monk is also civic-minded. He runs for the de facto mayor of the Five Points, wins, and puts aside his cudgel to have a civilized chat with his sworn enemy, Bill the Butcher. Instead of chatting civilly, Bill sinks an axe into Monk's back. The lesson here: Affability is all well and good, but always be prepared for a little murder.

In *28 Days Later . . .*, Gleeson plays Frank, who's trying to keep himself safe from zombie-like plague victims. In a world gone mad, Frank is touchingly affable toward fellow survivors Jim and Selena—treating them like they're long-lost relatives visiting for Christmas and not total strangers in fear of their lives. Soon enough, Frank gets infected with Rage, going from affability to murderousness in about twenty seconds. Right up until the moment when his eyes turn all red and scary and he goes to tear off a piece of his beloved daughter with his own teeth, we loved Gleeson.

Far and Away Social Club Policeman **1992**	*The Butcher Boy* Father Bubbles **1999**	*Gangs of New York* Walter "Monk" McGinn **2002**

Braveheart Hamish Campbell **1995**	*Artificial Intelligence: A.I.* Lord Johnson-Johnson **2001**

Jon Gries

Stats: **MULTI-ETHNIC**

BALD

VILLAIN

AS SEEN ON TV

HEY! IT'S THAT
WEASEL!

The second season of *24* involved the efforts of Jack Bauer (Kiefer Sutherland) to infiltrate an antigovernment militia group. Jack got involved in some pretty heavy shit to find his way to the big boss, Wald, The Big Bad! But if Wald was so big and scary and important, why was he played by Jon Gries?

Wald is several rungs up the criminal ladder from the sorts of minor scumbags Gries usually plays. Crooks? Sure. And losers. And crooked losers. But crooked losers like Dylan's heroin dealer on *90210*. And as for being in charge of anything . . . well, Jon Gries can handle your rickshaw (*Seinfeld*) or chauffeur a van full of illegal aliens (*Men in Black*). Only when *24*'s supposedly formidable Wald gets scared shitless and blows his brains out does it become clear that Wald is, after all, a textbook Jon Gries role.

Gries has developed a sideline, in recent years, playing a weasel of a different kind: yes, lawyers. In *Twin Falls Idaho*, Gries advised a prostitute who'd been hired for a naughty weekend by a pair of conjoined twins. On *ER*, he defended Sally Field from commitment to a psychiatric institution. But it's fitting that he played a criminal capo on *24*: If Wald had to be a towering figure who wouldn't live up to his hype, selling out his associates and dying unmourned, Jon Gries was the man for the job.

Helter Skelter William Garretson **1976**	*Real Genius* Lazlo Hollyfeld **1985**	*Napoleon Dynamite* Uncle Rico **2004**
Joysticks King Vidiot **1983**	*The Rundown* Harvey **2003**	

HEY! IT'S THAT GUY!

Luis Guzman

VILLAIN

HEY! IT'S THAT UGLY HOOD WHO MAY IN FACT BE AN UNDERCOVER COP!

POSSE MEMBER

WIG/PROSTHESIS USE

Lately, Luis Guzman seems to have been trying to play upstanding citizens: cops (*The Bone Collector* and *Confidence*), an earnest plumbing-supplies warehouse employee (*Punch-Drunk Love*), a game-show contestant (*Magnolia*).

But we remember and love him best for all his crooks. Guzman plays both legitimately scary criminals (*Oz*) and entertainingly bumbling ones (*Out of Sight*). Somewhere in the middle falls Cesar Pescador in the memorable early *Law & Order* episode "Heaven": Guzman's Cesar is an illegal immigrant at the center of an arson-for-hire case. Though chillingly effective at his task, he escapes neither discovery nor injury, and learns that crime doesn't pay—getting a nasty infection from having gasoline-soaked evidence buried in your flesh.

Because of Guzman's ability to move between enforcing the law and breaking it, criminals who admit Guzman into their headquarters need to be on their guard. If Miguel Ferrer (page 160) had been a little more suspicious of Guzman in *Traffic*, their characters both might have stayed alive until the closing credits. Instead, both get killed by the cartel's assassin. But at least they had some laughs before their deaths; Guzman's Ray tells a hell of a joke, and "playing" in a big bin of plastic balls is always a good time.

Carlito's Way
Pachanga
1993

Oz
Raoul "El Cid" Hernandez
1998–2000

The Count of Monte Cristo
Jacopo the Maggot, Monte Cristo's Valet
2002

House of Buggin'
Various Characters
1995

The Limey
Eduardo Roel
1999

James Hong

ICONIC ROLE

HEY! IT'S THAT ELEGANT
EVIL MASTERMIND!

Not only is James Hong an estimable and admirable Hey! It's That Guy! in his own right, but along with Victor Wong (page 61) and Al Leong (page 120), he forms a holy trinity of Asian villains. Between these three gentlemen, you've covered roughly 99 percent of the roles available to Asian actors in Hollywood. You've got your martial-arts assassin (that would be Leong), your crazy old wise man who sits in his cluttered curio shop in Chinatown (that would be Wong), and then, of course, your cool, calculating, mastermind type, who's elegant and slightly effeminate and ultimately not to be trusted. And that would be James Hong.

Conveniently, you can see all three actors playing their trademark roles in one super-fantastic movie: 1986's *Big Trouble in Little China*. Hong, for his part, is well known for this role, along with two others: 1) Hannibal Chew, Eyemaker, a.k.a. the guy who gets his own eyes squashed in *Blade Runner*; and 2) the maitre d' at the Chinese food restaurant in that brilliant early episode of *Seinfeld*, a.k.a. the "another five, ten minutes" guy.

With just these three roles alone, Hong has left an irrefutable mark on the culture. And so, James Hong, we salute you. Though we do it from a distance, as we fear that, if we got too close to you, you'd stab us with a poison-tipped chopstick.

Chinatown Kahn **1974**		*Tango & Cash* Quan **1989**		*Operation Dumbo Drop* Y B'ham **1995**
	The Golden Child Doctor Hong **1986**		*Tank Girl* Che'tsai **1995**	

Ricky Jay

DOUBLE THREAT

POSSE MEMBER

AWARD NOMINEE

HEY! IT'S THAT SLY, BEARDED
CON MAN!

It all started when we were watching *Mystery Men*. And we spotted this guy who was playing Captain Amazing's cynical agent—a rotund man with a trim beard and a vocal delivery that was equal parts laconic and sardonic: Let's call it "lardonic." And we wondered where we'd seen him before.

We soon ascertained that this was Ricky Jay, and we'd seen him as the quiz-show producer in *Magnolia*, the porn-film crew member in *Boogie Nights*, and Campbell Scott's ill-fated best friend in *The Spanish Prisoner*. We also, quite by accident, ascertained that Mr. Jay is a world-famous magician.

In fact, Ricky Jay is considered one of the half-dozen best, if not *the* best, sleight-of-hand magicians on the planet. He is also an obsessive collector of, and respected scholar on, rare magic books and artifacts, and he's an expert on the history of prestidigitation. He's also listed in the *Guinness Book of World Records* because he can throw a playing card 190 feet at a speed of 90 miles an hour. Discovering this about the guy in *Mystery Men* is kind of like discovering that Gedde Watanabe (page 180) is one the world's premier flautists and also has X-ray vision. Which is why we love this job.

House of Games
George/Vegas Man
1987

State and Main
Jack
2000

Heartbreakers
Dawson's Auctioneer
2001

Heist
Don "Pinky" Pincus
2001

Deadwood
Eddie Sawyer
2004

Al Leong

HEY! IT'S THAT DASTARDLY ASIAN KILLER/TERRORIST/SIDEKICK WITH A FU MANCHU!

DISTINCTIVE
FACIAL HAIR

Let's say you're putting together a crack gang of international terrorists to, say, hijack an office tower. You'll need an icy, silent, well-built Aryan type, preferably Austrian or German, and preferably wearing a turtleneck. You'll need a nerdy guy to circumvent alarm systems and . . . you know, hack into things. You'll also want to hire a huge African man who wears bandoliers and favors little knit caps and is always chewing on something. And, of course, you'll need an Asian guy, preferably one with a long Fu Manchu–style mustache.

In other words, you'll need Al Leong. You can trust Al Leong to do his job right, because he's been doing it right for so long, whether it was as "Wing Kong Hatchet Man" in *Big Trouble in Little China*, or Endo in *Lethal Weapon*, or "Gunman" in *The Replacement Killers*, or "Man in Croc-Pit Bar" in *The Perfect Weapon*, or, our personal favorite, as Uli in *Die Hard* (the one who steals a chocolate bar from a candy case before mowing down a team of bumbling SWAT guys).

Some contrarians point to his non-Asian-killer work, such as "Photographer" in *She's Having a Baby* or Genghis Khan in *Bill & Ted's Excellent Adventure*. But really, that latter role says everything you need to know about Al Leong: Even in a stoner comedy, he gets to play the ultimate Asian bad-ass.

They Live! Asian Revolutionary **1988**	*Escape from L.A.* Hershey's **1996**	*The Scorpion King* Asian Training Master **2002**
Beverly Hills Cop III Car Mechanic **1994**	*The Replacement Killers* Gunman **1998**	

Delroy Lindo

Stats:

AWARD NOMINEE

BALD

VILLAIN

PERIOD PIECE

HEY! IT'S THAT BIG, SCARY
CRIME BOSS!

We are outraged that Delroy Lindo is back to being a Hey! It's That Guy! An actor of his caliber shouldn't have to prostitute himself in a puddle of cinematic dribble like *Gone in Sixty Seconds* or *The One*.

We've seen him outperform megastar John Travolta (in *Get Shorty*) and wipe the floor with fine young actor yet charisma-free Tobey Maguire (in *The Cider House Rules*). But the only time he's ever been rewarded with critical acclaim was when he played a jovial but ultimately menacing gangster in *Clockers*.

So in effect, every outrage visited upon Delroy Lindo stems from a single cause: There isn't enough room in Hollywood to accommodate the many talented, nonwhite actors, which leaves Delroy Lindo—along with Alfre Woodard, Isaiah Washington (page 60), Debbi Morgan, Bill Nunn (page 163), Harry Lennix, and countless others—taking fourth billing, and glad to get it.

We wish we could travel back in time to 1994 and tell Quentin Tarantino to cast Delroy Lindo as Jules Winnfield, because if he had, the world would be a very different place today. With that in mind: You can now catch Delroy Lindo on DVD in *The Core* as Dr. Ed "Braz" Brazzleton.

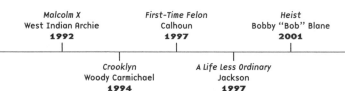

Malcolm X	*First-Time Felon*	*Heist*
West Indian Archie	Calhoun	Bobby "Bob" Blane
1992	**1997**	**2001**

Crooklyn	*A Life Less Ordinary*
Woody Carmichael	Jackson
1994	**1997**

Peter Stormare

Stats:

HEY! IT'S THAT SCANDINAVIAN/RUSSIAN ENFORCER!

Europeans must think that North Americans are deaf or dumb. How else to explain the fact that Swedish actor Peter Stormare has played so many Germans (*The Big Lebowski*) and Russians (*Armagoddon*)? The rationale must be that any "Continental" accent is indistinguishable from any other; all those foreigners are the same anyway, right?

Peter Stormare's prodigious height, deep voice, and stoned delivery combined to make his Gaear Grimsrud, in *Fargo*, an indelible memory. While the start of the movie casts Gaear as the laconic muscle behind Steve Buscemi's (page 108) bug-eyed, hopped-up-on-goofballs Carl Showalter, Stormare adds increasingly disturbing layers to the role as the movie progresses. While Carl runs around Minneapolis trying to chase down Jerry Lundegaard, Gaear takes the initiative to murder Jerry's wife.

Peter Stormare is probably a perfectly nice man in real life. But if we ever met him, we would have a hard time forgetting the image of him desultorily eating canned foods and gasping at a development in his soap opera while a woman lies dead on the floor a few feet away from him. At least in that role, he actually got to play a Swede.

The Lost World: Jurassic Park
Dieter Stark
1997

Chocolat
Serge Muscat
2000

Constantine
Satan, the 1st of the Fallen
2005

Dancer in the Dark
Jeff
2000

Minority Report
Dr. Solomon Eddie
2002

Brian Thompson

HEY! IT'S THAT MENACING
MUSCLEHEAD!

Stats: VILLAIN

STRAIGHT-TO-VIDEO

In the 1980s, Dolph Lundgren was often thought of as the poor man's Arnold Schwarzenegger. What, then, must it be like to be the poor man's Dolph Lundgren?

Make no mistake: That's not a slight on Brian Thompson. For starters, Brian Thompson could pick us up, break us into two pieces, stick wads of cotton on either end of those pieces, and clean out his ears with us. So, no slights here.

More importantly, we love Brian Thompson. He first came to our attention as the villainous Night Slasher in *Cobra*, the '80s-era action flick that hinged on the idea that Sylvester Stallone (as Lt. Marion "Cobra" Cobretti) could actually best Brian Thompson in a fistfight, which is, of course, absurd. Thompson went on to become a glowering, muscle-bound stalwart of low-rent action films, such as *Mortal Kombat: Annihilation*, *Commando Squad*, *Pass the Ammo*, and *Are You Talkin' to Me?*

And are we glad those movies exist? Ho, boy, yes we are. And, thus, we are glad for Brian Thompson, who's selflessly tackled such roles as "Second Thug," Hercules, and Saber. May we take this opportunity to point out that if your résumé includes a character named Saber, then you have done something very, very right in your career.

The Terminator Punk **1984**	*Alien Nation* Trent Porter **1988**	*Joe Dirt* Buffalo Bob **2001**
Three Amigos! German's Other Friend **1986**	*Dragonheart* Brok **1996**	

Danny Trejo

HEY! IT'S THAT
FREQUENTLY INCARCERATED
BAD-ASS!

If you recognize Danny Trejo, it's probably because 1) you've seen *Con Air*, *From Dusk Till Dawn*, *Heat*, or any of a number of similar films in which a certain tattooed bad-ass has played a prominent role, or 2) you once spent a long stretch in prison. Or, possibly, both. When you're in prison, you have a lot of time on your hands, and so you probably watch a lot of movies. Then again, we're guessing that, on movie night in prison, they don't show you *Con Air*.

But we digress.

Trejo was in prison himself, and we're not talking speeding tickets: He served time in San Quentin for armed robbery and drug offenses. Now he's an actor who often plays guys who are in prison. Name a film with a prison in it, and chances are Danny Trejo was in it too: *Lock Up*, *Deadlock*, and *Penitentiary III*, for example. Often, his characters are simply identified as "Prisoner" or "Prison Inmate" or "Tough Prisoner #1."

Trejo has played other characters, of course, in other films, but all have been bad-asses: characters like Razor Charlie or Uncle Machete or Sharkey

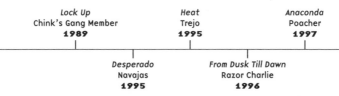

Lock Up
Chink's Gang Member
1989

Heat
Trejo
1995

Anaconda
Poacher
1997

Desperado
Navajas
1995

From Dusk Till Dawn
Razor Charlie
1996

or Jumpy or Scarface. When you have more than one character on your résumé who's named after a kind of lethal blade, then chances are, you're a bad-ass. Danny Trejo, for his part, is the personification of bad-ass. Not only was he in San Quentin, he was the boxing champion of San Quentin, for crying out loud! The king of beating up other bad-asses!

You might wonder if playing so many prisoners is hard for someone who has himself been a real-life prisoner.

We suspect the only thing he finds "hard" about playing a bad-ass in the movies is holding himself back from beating the living crap out of the other actors, as they prance around the set trying to act all bad-ass and fake-shooting at each other with their fake guns. We think that Danny Trejo probably laughs himself silly when he looks around some prison set and thinks that he now gets paid oodles of money to do pretty much exactly what he used to do every day for free. Now *that's* bad-ass.

HEY! IT'S CHAPTER SEVEN: THE HIDEOUT

Con Air
Johnny "Johnny-23" Baca
1997

Once Upon a Time in Mexico
Cucuy
2003

XXX
El Jefe
2002

Anchorman: The Legend of Ron Burgundy
Bartender
2004

Tensions are always running high in the hospital; after all, lives are on the line every day. It takes a special kind of person to cope with the pressure while still offering the best possible care. Some nurses and doctors manage to maintain their professional detachment and tend to their patients—from wacky old grannies in the geriatric ward to bitter young cancer sufferers counting down their last few days in oncology—with gentleness and sensitivity. Others (many

HEY! IT'S CHAPTER EIGHT:
THE HOSPITAL

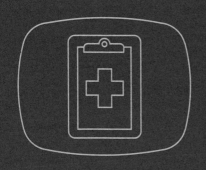

others) have a signature tough-love approach, which can yield even better results. And speaking of results, the hospital is home to the brilliant medical professional whose total lack of people skills sent him to a life in clinical research — are there hidden depths of feeling beneath that cold, prickly exterior? Only his ever-insightful therapist knows for sure.

Ellen Albertini Dow

Stats: HALL OF FAME

HEY! IT'S THAT
SASSY GRANNY!

ICONIC ROLE

AS SEEN ON TV

Sassy old people are funny. They just are. Put sunglasses on an old lady, get her to start rapping, and what have you got? Comedy, that's what.

When people talk about late-life blossoming, they mention Grandma Moses, who painted her first painting at 70, or Pauline Kael, who landed her job at *The New Yorker* at 48. No one talks about Albertini Dow, who didn't earn her first screen credit until age 68, when she played a geriatric serial killer in an episode of the new *Twilight Zone* series.

She's worked consistently since, playing sassy, wacky, crazy, and/or goofy grannies; most notably, she was the rapping granny in **The Wedding Singer**. Her cameo in the trailer ("I said a hip-hop, the hippie to the hippie, to the hip-hip-hop, and you don't stop") sent roughly half of the nation's moviegoers into hysterics and the other half into paroxysms of eye-rolling.

Yet Albertini Dow raps on—and rocks on—as such sassy grannies as Disco Dottie in **54**, Mrs. Mackenzie in **Ready to Rumble**, and Grandma Manilow in **Road Trip**. As such, she's arguably become America's favorite sassy granny. Who better to liven up the old folks' home or the geriatric ward than a rapping granny? It's smiles all around!

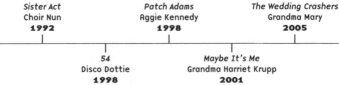

Sister Act
Choir Nun
1992

Patch Adams
Aggie Kennedy
1998

The Wedding Crashers
Grandma Mary
2005

54
Disco Dottie
1998

Maybe It's Me
Grandma Harriet Krupp
2001

Bruce Altman

Stats: AS SEEN ON TV

HEY! IT'S THAT NASAL-VOICED, POSSIBLY CROOKED
PSYCHIATRIST!

Your typical therapist cares about your problems, or acts as though he does. But Bruce Altman don't play that. His voice is very nasal, which makes everything he says sound like a distracted afterthought: "I may be paid, by you, to sit here and listen to you, but I am thinking about my boat."

This blasé attitude was a total put-on in *Matchstick Men*. In fact, Altman's Dr. Klein was extremely interested in everything his patient, Roy Waller (Nicolas Cage), had to tell him. It was his job to collect information in order to customize a con. So this role proved that Bruce Altman really can act like he cares—but only about running his own game on a troubled weirdo. (A cynic would say that sounds pretty much like what all therapists do.)

Sometimes he's on the periphery of criminal activity—as the inattentive father of a sexually abused boy (*L.I.E.*) or a mark for a real-estate scam (*Glengarry Glen Ross*). Other times, he's just plain dirty, as when he played Mob in-law Harv Beigal on an early two-part *Law & Order* (married to Christine Baranski [page 49], no less!). Even in *Changing Lanes*, in which he plays a lawyer representing a bereaved daughter fighting to preserve her father's philanthropic trust fund, the only thing that can redeem him is to pit him against Ben Affleck's Chief Smarmtroller. And, dude, that match-up would even make Roy Cohn look good.

Cop Land Counselor Burt Handel **1997**		L.I.E. Marty Blitzer **2001**		Matchstick Men Dr. Klein **2003**
	The Object of My Affection Dr. Goldstein **1998**		Changing Lanes Joe Kaufman **2002**	

Amy Aquino

Stats: **MULTI-ETHNIC**

HEY! IT'S THAT CRABBY HEAD OF
OBSTETRICS!

PERIOD PIECE

One of the most prevalent—and justified—complaints about the glut of teen-targeted one-hour dramas on The WB is that the shows' protagonists are invariably self-involved whiners.

Felicity counteracted those critics by introducing a tertiary character to kick the protagonist in the ass: Dr. Toni Pavone, Felicity's shrink. Keri Russell couldn't have pulled off Felicity's gradual yet believable emotional transformation over the course of the series were it not for the work of the subtle TV veteran Amy Aquino.

Aquino has turned up on some of the most acclaimed shows on TV, like *Freaks & Geeks*, *The Larry Sanders Show*, and *The West Wing*. Her most widely seen recurring role is as Dr. Janet Coburn, the obstetrician on *ER*. She first appeared in "Love's Labor Lost," in which Mark Greene is responsible for a pregnant woman's death; Coburn calls him incompetent, and for that we will always love her.

When Aquino was cast in a leading role, it was on a show too good to survive on television: *Brooklyn Bridge*. We like her better tossing off zingers from the sidelines in her trademark deadpan tone. If she were still starring on *Brooklyn Bridge*, she wouldn't have had time to take Felicity down a peg or ten. And we'd all be the poorer for it.

Brooklyn Bridge Phyllis Berger Silver **1991**	*Crossing Jordan* Det. Lois Carver **2001**	*The Singing Detective* Nurse Nozhki **2003**

Picket Fences Dr. Joanna "Joey" Diamond **1995–1996**	*Everybody Loves Raymond* Peggy **2002–2004**

Viola Davis

Stats: **AWARD WINNER**

HEY! IT'S THAT
HARD-EYED NURSE/
SOCIAL WORKER!

AS SEEN ON TV

PERIOD PIECE

Viola Davis has the no-bullshit look of a smart, tough woman who could seriously flatten anyone who makes the mistake of getting on her bad side. As such, she often plays professionals in responsible positions of authority—doctors, nurses, social workers, cops, lawyers, and others who have power over your life.

Yet Davis is always the voice of reason and good sense. Like when she's playing a doctor sharing a spaceship with George Clooney, trying to talk his crazy ass down from the ledge when he becomes convinced that the illusions generated by the mysterious titular planet *Solaris* are real. Or when she's a social worker who's the first person to see that time is running out for teenage drug abuser Erika Christensen to deal with her addiction in *Traffic*. Or when she's playing nearly silent maid Sybil in *Far from Heaven*. Davis's innate authority there cannot be denied: She communicates her unease about the biracial relationship in which Julianne Moore's Cathy is getting involved with her strong, silent, watchful gaze.

In fact, we hoped that the naïve, breathless Cathy would finally overstep the bounds of her relationship in some serious and permanent way, forcing Sybil to plow her one in the face—or at least shame her, with a devastating speech, into shutting up forever.

The Substance of Fire Nurse **1996**	*City of Angels* Nurse Lynnette Peeler **2000**	*Antwone Fisher* Eva **2002**
	Out of Sight Moselle Miller **1998**	*Far from Heaven* Sybil **2002**

Glenn Fitzgerald

Stats:

**HEY! IT'S THAT
CRANKY YET HEROIC
TERMINAL PATIENT!**

Glenn Fitzgerald's roles fall into two distinct categories: attractive, slightly dull young men and greasy, antisocial creeps. Fitzgerald's most iconic role in the former category is as Olivia Williams's sweet, unassuming coworker, Sean, in *The Sixth Sense*. Because Sean is a polite, upstanding fellow, it took a few moments for us to recognize him—Sean is a 180-degree turn from the role for which we love him best: Lonnie in *Flirting with Disaster*. After enduring all the angst of Mel's (Ben Stiller) search for his biological parents, the Schlichtings (Lily Tomlin and Alan Alda), we learn that they've produced another child, Lonnie, all combed-forward hair and belly shirt, flouncing about the house broadcasting his resentment toward his long-lost brother. Lonnie is a delight.

Jeffrey Norman, Fitzgerald's character in the underrated *Series 7: The Contenders*—a scripted film presented in the form of a nonexistent reality show—is a spiritual sibling to Lonnie, if Lonnie were a terminally ill closeted gay man who was then selected by the government to murder several people including his now-pregnant high-school girlfriend. From Jeffrey, it was just a short step to Aaron, the bitter cancer patient that Nate (Peter Krause) counsels through his own funeral planning on *Six Feet Under*. Someone get this kid some vitamins before he's hired to play a guy with Ebola.

The Ice Storm Neil Conrad **1997**	*The Sixth Sense* Sean **1999**	*Six Feet Under* Aaron Buchbinder **2002**
A Price Above Rubies Mendel Horowitz **1998**	*The Believer* Drake **2001**	

Margo Martindale

Stats: AS SEEN ON TV

HEY! IT'S THAT
SARDONIC NURSE!

PERIOD PIECE

Margo Martindale will not take any crap from anyone. Her East Texas accent makes her sound as if her patients' ailments are supremely boring; no matter what manner of histrionics they might attempt, she remains unimpressed. Her heavyset figure makes her seem sturdy and maternal and all those other stereotypes one associates with larger, older women. She looks like someone who'd be at home matter-of-factly clearing away dinner trays or administering medication via injection—along with a jaded quip—in a patient's ass.

Martindale must enjoy playing nurses, because she keeps taking such roles—in **Sabrina**, **In Dreams**, and others. In keeping with the sardonic/nurturing mojo she has working, Martindale plays a psychiatrist in **Marvin's Room**, a psychologist in **The Human Stain**, a nun in **Dead Man Walking**, and a babysitter in **The Hours**. (She's also chilling in **Million Dollar Baby**, in a complete deviation from type, playing a horrendous trailer-trash mom.)

Checking Sandra Bullock into her rehab center in **28 Days**, Martindale manages to cut her down to size in less than five minutes, informing her that she'll be carrying her own luggage, and ferreting out Vicodin concealed in Bullock's bag. Martindale spends most of the movie planted behind the rehab center's reception desk, and still displays more charisma than Mike O'Malley and Azura Skye combined, doing so with equal parts nursing and sardonicism. It's her way.

Lonesome Dove Plump Ogallala Tart **1989**	*28 Days* Betty **2000**	*Million Dollar Baby* Earline Fitzgerald **2004**
	The Firm Nina Huff **1993**	*The Laramie Project* Trish Steger **2002**

J. K. Simmons

HEY! IT'S THAT HOSPITAL
PSYCHIATRIST
WHO COULD BE A PSYCHOPATH!

There are certain character actors who seem to pop up in every other movie; then there are character actors like J. K. Simmons. Simmons hasn't appeared in a wide range of roles, but the parts he has played tend to leave an impression. Sometimes literally. Sometimes in the shape of a swastika on your ass cheek.

Take, for example, his signature role, that of prisoner #92G110, better known as Vern Schillinger, the resident Nazi psychopath on HBO's *Oz*. We'd venture a guess that if Schillinger had turned up in, say, an FBI movie starring Jodie Foster, he'd already be ensconced in pop culture's annals of classic villainy, right up there with Mr. Hannibal Lecter himself.

You may also recognize Simmons from his more high-profile role as J. Jonah Jameson in the *Spider-Man* movies, in which he gleefully alternates between chewing on a cigar butt and chewing on the scenery. But Simmons also has a quieter, slightly less psychopathic, side: Consider, for example, his recurring role on *Law & Order*, in which he plays Dr. Emil Skoda. Skoda is a sardonic, cynical criminal psychologist, cool like lemonade, and he sometimes seems like he might have ended up as a criminal psychopath himself, if he hadn't done so well on the MCAT.

The First Wives Club	Autumn in New York	The Ladykillers
Federal Marshal	Dr. Tom Grandy	Garth Pancake
1996	**2000**	**2004**

The Cider House Rules	The Gift
Frank Perry	Sheriff Pearl Johnson
1999	**2000**

Stellan Skarsgard

HEY! IT'S THAT BRILLIANT BUT HIGH-STRUNG FOREIGN PSYCHOLOGIST!

Stats: AWARD NOMINEE

FOREIGNER

Stellan Skarsgard has been living a double life. In one, he's a major movie star who found fame early, as a teen, in the well-received TV series *Bombi Bitt Och Jag*. (By the way, this first life takes place in Sweden.) This Stellan Skarsgard stars in Lars Von Trier films such as *Breaking the Waves*, *Dancer in the Dark*, and *Dogville*.

In his second life, Stellan Skarsgard is also a movie star—of sorts. This Stellan Skarsgard played the brainy, high-strung foreigner opposite Robert De Niro in the 1998 film *Ronin*; the brilliant but testy math professor in *Good Will Hunting*; and the high-strung shark bait in *Deep Blue Sea*.

He's also done a handful of films he'd no doubt prefer to forget (or prefer that we forget): *The Glass House*, for example, in which he played the villain, Terry Glass. (Get it? It was his house.) He lent a mumbling, virtually unrecognizable turn to *King Arthur*, as the head Gaul. He also starred as the young Father Merrin in the whose-bad-idea-was-this? prequel to *The Exorcist* titled *Exorcist: The Beginning*.

Skarsgard is supremely talented, and in true, stalwart, character-actor style, he's never less than good, even in films in which he looks slightly embarrassed. Thankfully, many American audiences mistake this look for high-strung foreignness, which suits his purposes just fine.

Amistad
Tappan
1997

Ronin
Gregor
1998

Exorcist: The Beginning
Father Merrin
2004

Good Will Hunting
Gerald Lambeau
1997

Dogville
Chuck
2003

Joey Slotnick

HEY! IT'S THAT NEBBISHY,
WISEACRE SURGEON
WITH A VENGEFUL SCALPEL!

Slotnick.

Roll it around in your mouth. Notice how close it is to "Snotlick." Imagine how this must have affected his childhood. Now whisper it, as tenderly as a lover's promise:

Slotnick.

Joey Slotnick first came to our attention when he played the irritating sidekick to the even more irritating Jonathan Silverman on the supremely irritating 1995 NBC sitcom *The Single Guy*. Slotnick was, it should be noted, the least irritating of the cast—though this is akin to being handed a box full of stool samples from various members of the animal kingdom and having to choose which one you'd most like to eat.

Fast-forward to 2000, when Slotnick surfaced again, this time in the terrible, *Invisible-Man*-as-sexual-predator movie, ***Hollow Man***. Here, Slotnick upped the nebbish ante as a nerdy computer techie, a choice that played solidly off his Muppet-esque good looks. (Slotnick, with his ovoid head and

A League of Their Own
Doris Fan #2
1992

Twister
Joey
1996

The Single Guy
Sam Sloan
1995–1997

Pirates of Silicon Valley
Steve Wozniak
1999

corona-like fringe of curls, looks a bit like Jeremy Piven, as reimagined by Jim Henson.)

Later that same year, Slotnick starred on **Boston Public**, David E. Kelley's high-school drama/paean to braless teen girls. El Slotnick played the Poindexter-ish teacher Milton Buttle, who was eventually run out of school for having an affair with one of the aforementioned braless teens.

Then in 2003, Hurricane Slotnick touched down on the saucy cable show **Nip/Tuck**. His character, Dr. Merril Bobolit, is a nebbishy and unscrupulous plastic surgeon who uses his wealth and power to exact revenge on all those who've mocked him (memories of "Snotlick," no doubt)—or, at least, on their proxies, in the form of comatose women whom he slices up with scalpels.

With this role, Slotnick established his specialty—his Slotniche, if you will. All hail the king of the wiseacre nerd, the ambitious nebbish, the vengeful Poindexter.

All hail Slotnick.

Hollow Man
Frank Chase
2000

Alias
CIA Agent Steven Haladki
2002

Boston Public
Milton Buttle
2000–2001

Nip/Tuck
Dr. Merril Bobolit
2003

Who finished the coffee without putting on another pot? Was it the smarmy bastard of a junior executive who has no real skills but got a good management job because his uncle is a VP? Was it the frumpy secretary who always seems to be hatching some kind of hare-brained scheme to blackmail people higher up the corporate ladder? Was it that squirrelly guy who won't shut up about his stapler? Was it the obvious white-collar criminal who never talks to

THE OFFICE

anyone? Was it that absolutely huge dude with the gigantic neck that we always get to change the bottle on the water cooler? No. It wasn't any of them. It was the worst imaginable boss in the world, who's always drawling out his instructions in the most annoyingly protracted way possible—and he's drinking that last cup of coffee *right now*! We *hate* that guy!

Dylan Baker

HEY! IT'S THAT CLEAN-CUT, OCCASIONALLY CREEPY
WHITE-COLLAR GUY!

Dylan Baker is fortunate to look the part of the upper-middle-class everyman; he's already racked up a list of credits that outnumber his years on Earth. Like any Hey! It's That Guy! worth his salt, Baker's played an array of army guys, cops, doctors, lawyers, politicians, and even a couple of priests.

Good as Baker is at playing an actual normal guy, he's even better at playing a seemingly normal guy whose unflappable exterior conceals all manner of depravity. Sometimes, he's just a little bit depraved—as in *Changing Lanes*, in which he played the hacker who wiped out Samuel L. Jackson's credit rating.

But then there's *Happiness*. Leave it to writer-director Todd Solondz to create the ultimate Average White Guy with Unfathomable Depths of Depravity, a.k.a. Bill Maplewood. Baker takes this absolutely despicable character—a suburban therapist-cum-pedophile who drugs and molests

Planes, Trains & Automobiles
Owen
1987

The Long Walk Home
Tunker Thompson
1990

Love Potion No. 9
Prince Geoffrey
1992

Happiness
Bill Maplewood
1998

Thirteen Days
Robert McNamara,
Secretary of Defense
2000

his sons' friends when they sleep over at his house—and manages the seemingly impossible: He makes him sort of sympathetic. Baker's performance is so thoughtful and compelling and tragic, even, that we are invested enough to want to follow his journey to its (inevitable) conclusion, rather than abandoning the movie midway through it to take a long, cleansing shower. The movie is hardly the feel-good story of any year, but the whole thing pretty much rests on Baker's ability to make the degenerate Maplewood a three-dimensional character rather than a melodramatic monster.

Baker was also part of the scenery behind Tom Hanks in ***Road to Perdition***. There may be a parallel universe in which the actor who brought Bill Maplewood to life would have won back-to-back Oscars while the one who portrayed *Forrest Gump* would be a lowly supporting player; sadly, that is not the universe in which we live.

Changing Lanes
Finch
2002

Road to Perdition
Alexander Rance
2002

Head of State
Martin Geller
2003

Spider-Man 2
Dr. Curt Connors
2004

Kinsey
Alan Gregg
2004

Gary Cole

HEY! IT'S THAT TORTUROUSLY
IRRITATING BOSS!

Gary Cole has played über-dads in movies like *I'll Be Home for Christmas* and the Ur-dad in the big-screen *Brady Bunch* adaptations. The smooth cadence and soothing timbre of his voice made him an eerie dead ringer (vocally, anyway) for the late Robert Reed's Mike Brady, and he, more than any of the movie's other performers, really went the whole nine yards in filling out those '70s duds and embodying the irony-free attitude the film required. Rare is the actor who can don the white man's Afro and behave as if he doesn't notice it. Gary Cole is such an actor.

But then there's the other Gary Cole—the menacing creep in *American Gothic*, the homicidal maniac in *Fatal Vision* and *A Simple Plan*. This Gary Cole uses that same smooth cadence and soothing timbre to finesse his way past a victim's natural defenses . . . then kills him. Or at least makes

Midnight Caller
Jack "Nighthawk" Killian
1988–1991

*The Brady Bunch Movie/
A Very Brady Sequel/
The Brady Bunch
in the White House*
Mike Brady
1995/1996/2002

Office Space
Bill Lumbergh
1999

American Gothic
Sheriff Lucas Black
1995–1996

A Simple Plan
Neil Baxter
1998

HEY! IT'S THAT GUY!

him feel as if Cole might kill him—that his air of menace is very real and that the fear he causes is legitimate. Sure, his face seems bland and friendly. But he's an enigma!

As if to integrate the two dominant themes on his résumé, Gary Cole played the villain in the bitterly hilarious cult hit *Office Space*. As office antagonist Bill Lumbergh, Cole delivered his lines—painfully familiar to anyone who'd ever toiled under a middle manager with a Napoleon complex— with a bored detachment meant to disguise his acute awareness of the petty power he wielded over his drones' very existence (at work if nowhere else). Lumbergh represents the perfect marriage of Cole's bland dispassion and his steely malevolence—and hence, it is Gary Cole's signature role.

Fatal Vision
Capt. Jeffrey MacDonald, M.D.
2001

One Hour Photo
Bill Owens
2002

*Dodgeball:
A True Underdog Story*
Cotton McKnight
2004

*Harvey Birdman,
Attorney at Law*
Harvey Birdman
2001–

The West Wing
Bill Russell
2003–

Paul Giamatti

**HEY! IT'S THAT
HYPERTENSIVE SCREAMER/
SHAMBLING LIFER!**

While Paul Giamatti spent the early '90s building a solid CV of anonymous roles in big-budget films, it was not until the icy winter of 1997 that he turned in his first show-stopping performance. In the Howard Stern biopic **Private Parts**, Giamatti played Kenny Rushton, better known as Pig Vomit—the very worst kind of office jackass, imparting moronic edicts without any regard for maintaining civil relationships with his coworkers. We were sure Pig Vomit would be a star-making role for Giamatti—the kind that vaults an actor from being Jason Alexander in *Pretty Woman* to being Jason Alexander on *Seinfeld*.

The same year, Giamatti played an FBI technician in the modest cult hit **Donnie Brasco** but then opted for less showy roles—the nameless bellboy who smokes a cigarette with Julia Roberts in **My Best Friend's Wedding**; the control-room supervisor in **The Truman Show**; a soldier in **Saving Private Ryan**. In the HBO original movie **Winchell**, he starred opposite fellow well-

Private Parts
Kenny "Pig Vomit" Rushton
1997

Winchell
Herman Klurfeld
1998

If These Walls Could Talk 2
Ted Hedley
2000

The Negotiator
Rudy Timmons
1998

Man on the Moon
Bob Zmuda/Tony Clifton
1999

respected character actor Stanley Tucci, which is all well and good, but who ever got famous from a supporting role in an HBO movie? Elizabeth Mitchell? Vondie Curtis-Hall? Al Waxman?

Since Winchell, Giamatti has brought his likable, shambling screen presence to ensemble casts in movies both well regarded (***Cradle Will Rock***, ***The Negotiator***) and not (***Duets***, ***Tim Burton's Planet of the Apes***).

Finally, in 2003, Giamatti got his first and long-overdue chance to carry his own film. ***American Splendor***—in which Giamatti plays underground comic-book writer/file-clerk lifer in the Department of Veterans Affairs Harvey Pekar—won the Grand Jury Prize at Sundance and could, over time, do for Giamatti what *The Fugitive* did for Tommy Lee Jones. It landed him ***Sideways***, yet another role of the sort that leads to Hey! It's That Guy! breakout success stories . . . though not Oscar nominations, apparently. Damn you, The Academy!

Duets
Todd Woods
2000

Storytelling
Toby Oxman
2001

Big Fat Liar
Marty Wolf
2002

American Splendor
Harvey Pekar
2003

Sideways
Miles Raymond
2004

Judy Greer

AS SEEN ON TV

PERIOD PIECE

HEY! IT'S THAT GAWKY DORK/SKINNY, CONNIVING BITCH!

For the first third of *Jawbreaker*, Judy Greer is nerdy high schooler Fern, who had a homoerotic crush on Liz, the woman whose death kicks off the movie. To buy her silence about Liz's death, Liz's friends make Fern over into Vylette, a sexy siren.

Greer so ably embodied both Fern the dork and Vylette the diva that she's been doing nothing but those roles since.

Divas: See *Arrested Development*, in which Greer, as Kitty, George Sr.'s mistress, won't scruple to serve him in whatever way possible; and *13 Going on 30*, in which Greer plays a backstabbing brat of a glossy-chick-mag editor.

Dorks: See *What Women Want*, in which Greer's miserable office assistant has a cri de coeur that only Mel Gibson can hear, allowing him to prevent her suicide; and *The Wedding Planner*—working as J. Lo's assistant would make anyone want to blend into the background, assuming you didn't end up going on a killing spree.

Three Kings Cathy Daitch **1999**	*The Hebrew Hammer* Esther Bloomenbergansteinthal **2002**	*The Village* Kitty Walker **2004**
	Adaptation Alice the Waitress **2002**	*13 Going on 30* Lucy Wyman **2004**

Zach Grenier

Stats: BALD

HEY! IT'S THAT
GLOWERING BOSS!

VILLAIN

AS SEEN ON TV

Zach Grenier has such an effective screw-you glare that it's ironic he was cast as the ramrod office boss who gets trod all over by Edward Norton in *Fight Club*. Ironic, but not surprising: After all, Grenier, with his scowling brow, tersely set lips, and tractor-beam intensity, is the very personification of the office boss you really, really hate. He's the kind of malevolently banal overlord who's as much a part of office culture as cubicles, fluorescent tubes, Cathy mugs, and lukewarm cups of coffee.

Grenier barks orders and makes demands. He's got no time for excuses and never cracks a smile. It's no wonder, then, that when he's not playing cruel bosses, he's often playing hard-line military toughs or humorless lawmen like Carl Webb on *24* or Assistant FBI Director Bill Joy in *Swordfish*. There is, of course, no joy in Bill Joy. (And no joy in *Swordfish*, but that's another story.) So it's appropriate, then, that Grenier appeared in *Fight Club* as the stand-in for every manager or supervisor you ever wanted to tell to take a long walk off a short loading dock.

This is a man who once played super-Nazi Joseph Goebbels, for crying out loud. If he can tackle that, he can probably handle your shift supervisor, no matter how much of a jerk you think he is.

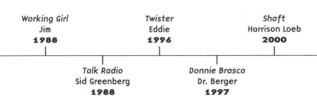

Working Girl Jim **1988**		*Twister* Eddie **1996**		*Shaft* Harrison Loeb **2000**
	Talk Radio Sid Greenberg **1988**		*Donnie Brasco* Dr. Berger **1997**	

HEY! IT'S CHAPTER NINE: THE OFFICE   147

John Michael Higgins

HEY! IT'S THAT VERY PROFESSIONAL
HOUSE COUNSEL!

If it hurt John Michael Higgins's career to piss off David Letterman by playing him in the 1996 HBO film *The Late Shift*, you'd never know it. Now, Higgins is doing really well for himself. He's guest-starred on some of our most beloved sitcoms, first on *Seinfeld*, and later haunting the halls of the Bluth Company, hiding behind pieces of furniture as a would-be house counsel on *Arrested Development*.

Higgins has also joined the Christopher Guest repertory company. In *A Mighty Wind*, Higgins is Terry Bohner, the absurdly tanned, earnest, pastel-clad, dorky frontman of *The New Main Street Singers*. But the greatest role of Higgins's career so far is as Scott Donlan in *Best in Show*. Scott and his partner, Stefan Vanderhoof (Michael McKean), are parents to an obscenely pampered purse dog. When they arrive at their hotel for the dog show, the desk clerk confirms, "We have you down for a queen," and Scott faux-indignantly replies, "What are you suggesting, my dear man?" Once the topic

The Late Shift
David Letterman
1996

Wag the Dog
John Levy
1997

Best in Show
Scott Donlan
2000

G.I. Jane
Chief of Staff
1997

Ally McBeal
Steven Milter
2000–2002

of payment arises, Scott dismissively turns his back and, with a wave of his hand in Stefan's direction, sniffs, "Talk to Daddy." Scott is a flaming queen. As such, he's got some over-the-top queenisms to express. But Higgins plays Scott much as he had played Letterman: as a character, not a caricature. Scott has a specific kind of dignity; to see him lead his dog in the show is to see some serious, world-class prancing and mincing.

Higgins then appeared in **La La Wood**, the film adaptation of *Primetime Glick*. It would have been easy there for every take to be overplayed to a near-vaudevillian degree. We hope Higgins shook that off by returning to **Harvey Birdman**, **Attorney at Law**, in which he voices Mentok the Mindtaker opposite such all-stars of deadpan comedy as Gary Cole (page 142) and Stephen Colbert (of *The Daily Show*). That is where our boy belongs: perfectly underplaying his role as a green-skinned psychic/judge in a cartoon courtroom. Because, you know, you wouldn't want a role like that to be played too "big."

A Mighty Wind Terry Bohner **2003**	*La La Wood* Andre Divine **2004**	*Boston Legal* Jerry Austin **2004**

Arrested Development Wayne Jarvis **2003**	*Blade: Trinity* Dr. Edgar Vance **2004**

Stephen Root

HEY! IT'S THAT
MUMBLING NEBBISH/
BLOWHARD BOSS!

PERIOD PIECE

You may know Stephen Root from his role as Jimmy James, the oddball station owner on the much-loved sitcom ***News Radio***. Or you may know him for his knockout role in the 1999 cult comedy ***Office Space***, in which he played the psychotic office nebbish, Milton Waddams, a disaffected, bespectacled mound who sat muttering to himself about the disappearance of his Swingline stapler. You may not, however, know that these two office archetypes were played by the same guy, so versatile is our Mr. Root.

Unlike most Hey! It's That Guy!s, Root doesn't have a signature niche. He can play almost anything. He's Lund, the squealing, blind radio station manager in ***O Brother, Where Art Thou?*** He's Gordon, the out-of-shape fitness nut in ***Dodgeball***. No matter the role, though, Root always brings a crackerjack sense of comic timing and a genius for off-kilter line readings. He's just damned funny.

In a perfect world, he would have his own sitcom. Then again, if he ever did get a starring sitcom vehicle, they'd probably make him play a divorced dad who suddenly inherits the rambunctious twin daughters of his recently deceased brother, and they wouldn't let him wear any funny glasses or fake blind eyeballs or spandex bicycle shorts. And that wouldn't really be a perfect world at all, now would it?

Crocodile Dundee II DEA Agent **1988**	*Bicentennial Man* Dennis Mansky, Head of NorthAm Robotics **1999**	*The Ladykillers* Fernand Gudge **2004**

	Ghost Detective Sergeant NYPD **1990**	*Finding Nemo* Bubbles the Yellow Fish **2003**	

Jay O. Sanders

Stats: AS SEEN ON TV

PERIOD PIECE

HEY! IT'S THAT BULL-NECKED
SALES MANAGER!

Jay O. Sanders has never been pigeonholed as a big dumb guy. The guys he plays are actually smart—like the climatologist in *The Day After Tomorrow*, or the D.A.'s investigator in *JFK*, or the FBI agent in *Kiss the Girls* and its sequel. Sanders's substantial physique works in concert with his sharp mind; it's no good if a brilliant investigative mind is housed inside a pencil-necked geek.

Sanders is also a love machine. Specifically, he's Dan, the big, sweet stud who proves to sad, bitter single mothers that they can, in fact, love again. In *Tumbleweeds*, Sanders is Dan Miller, officemate to Janet McTeer's Mary Jo. His technique here is to bond with Mary Jo's daughter over *Romeo and Juliet* (smart!). In *Music of the Heart*, he's Dan Paxton, a reporter who answers a personal ad for Roberta Guaspari (Meryl Streep) and helps her through a professional crisis (supportive!).

The boyfriends Sanders has played of late are not so much ideal as idealized, but so what? Some people are partial to screen heroes whose superpowers involve shooting spider silk out their wrists; others prefer the kind who do important stuff, like taking the kids out so their moms can take a nice bath. Sanders is the latter kind of superhero. Although, given his colossal figure, he's only a leotard away from being the former.

After MASH	For Richer or Poorer	Music of the Heart
Dr. Gene Pfeiffer	Samuel Yoder	Dan Paxton
1983	**1997**	**1999**

The MatchMaker	Tumbleweeds
Sen. John McGlory	Dan Miller
1997	**1999**

Nick Searcy

HEY! IT'S THAT POSSIBLY MALEVOLENT COWORKER!

BALD

VILLAIN

AS SEEN ON TV

Nick Searcy is your coworker. He's your boss. He's your president. He's that guy who hangs around the photocopier and seems, frankly, like a bit of a kiss-ass.

Searcy is the slightly out-of-shape highway patrolman who pulls you over and gives you a hard time just for the hell of it. He is Sheriff Rawlins in **The Fugitive**, who doesn't cotton to these big-city cops waltzin' in and thinking they can hijack his investigation. He looks slightly boring but also menacing. He is Hollywood's idea of what a regular guy looks like.

Searcy is the dorky but malevolent white guy running for president against Chris Rock in **Head of State**. Searcy is the district manager who comes by your cubicle at 4:45 on Friday and asks you to stick around for another few hours because he's getting heat about those unfinished reports. Searcy is not Zach Grenier (page 147), the guy who played Ed Norton's boss in *Fight Club*, though he looks very similar to him.

In fact, if Searcy looks familiar, it's not only because he's a Hey! It's That Guy!, but because he looks a lot like a bunch of other Hey! It's That Guy!s. Which makes him some sort of a Meta–Hey! It's That Guy! Suffice it to say, we like Nick Searcy because we never Meta–Hey! It's That Guy! we didn't like. Ba-da-boom! Thank you!

Days of Thunder Highway Patrol Officer **1990**	*Nell* Sheriff Todd Peterson **1994**	*Runaway Jury* Doyle **2003**
	Fried Green Tomatoes Frank Bennett **1991**	*One Hour Photo* Repairman **2002**

Stephen Tobolowsky

Stats:

HALL OF FAME

BALD

WIG/PROSTHESIS USE

HEY! IT'S THAT SPUTTERING
APPARATCHIK!

Stephen Tobolowsky is a wonderful actor, but his real genius is in his face: that doughy, slightly Seussian visage that lends itself perfectly to the portrayal of sputtering apparatchiks. He was born to play the clueless mayor, the harrumphing boss, the self-important studio head, just as James Rebhorn (page 98), with his gaunt, stern kisser, is perfectly sculpted to play vaguely menacing bureaucrats. And neither could dream of playing the other's roles. Who says nature doesn't have a plan?

In fact, as better-known stars become increasingly interchangeable—Dennis Quaid or Jeff Bridges? Brad Pitt or Matt Damon?—ask yourself this: Who could have played the irritating salesman Ned Ryerson in **Groundhog Day** better than Tobolowsky? Or the jittery pillar of the community/village racist Townley in **Mississippi Burning**? Or the muddled amnesiac Sammy Jankis in **Memento**? Or the spineless CBS toadie Eric Kluster in **The Insider**?

Yet does Tobolowsky get his proper respects? Hell, no! In not one but two of his film credits, he's miscredited as "Stephen Tobolowski"! Do you ever see a credit for "Matt Dramon"? Or "Dennis Quid"?

Seriously, people, let's get it right. Tobolowsky is a towering star, indispensable in a way that Matt Dramon or Dennis Quid could never be. And it's time we respected that.

Spaceballs Captain of the Guard **1987**	*Basic Instinct* Dr. Lamott **1992**	*Single White Female* Mitch Myerson **1992**
Thelma & Louise Max **1991**	*Sneakers* Dr. Werner Brandes **1992**	

Law and order: These aren't just the precepts that make civilization possible, they're the building blocks that drive an entire industry and keep thousands of character actors alive and well fed. And that's just one TV franchise! Yes, Hollywood loves a good cop show, but where would it be without cops? Look around the precinct and you'll see all the familiar types: the burly, good-natured desk sergeant (Hey, Sarge!); the hard-driving, unscrupulous D.A. who'll do

THE PRECINCT

anything to Slam-dunk! This! Case!; the shambling, disaffected partner to the glamorous homicide detective (actually, don't worry about him; he gets killed in the second reel). And just days before retirement! The irony! And don't cross that prison guard, the one with the iron stare. He's got a pillowcase full of oranges, and he knows what to do with them. And we don't mean hand them out as a midday snack, or squeeze them for mimosas. We mean beat you with them. Hard.

Gary Basaraba

Stats:

HEY! IT'S THAT JOLLY
DESK SERGEANT!

Every precinct needs a good cop and a bad cop. Gary Basaraba makes a very good good cop. (Dennis Franz, on the other hand, makes a good bad cop. Jim Belushi makes a bad bad cop—and a bad good cop, for that matter.) Gary Basaraba is the jolly, rotund sergeant who stands behind the desk, signs you in, and then asks if you want a warm-up on your java.

Basaraba, who's from Edmonton, Alberta, spent much of his early career playing the kinds of roles that jolly, rotund, balding actors usually play: genial Southern neighbors, bartenders, or Andrew the Apostle. You know, the usual. (Okay, maybe not that last one—though Basaraba did play Andrew in *The Last Temptation of Christ*. It's a shame Basaraba didn't play Barabbas.)

But he truly found his niche when he played Sgt. Richard Santaro, the affable desk sergeant on the short-lived cop show *Brooklyn South*. He's since played a police detective in *Unfaithful*, a police officer in *Boomtown*, and a police detective in the straight-to-video movie *K-9: P.I.*

In fact, Basaraba is so well-suited to play cops that he's like the funny friend who gets asked to be the best man at everyone's wedding. He should stop renting the cop uniform, and just invest in one for himself. Trust us: It will pay for itself in no time.

Fried Green Tomatoes Grady Kilgore **1991**	*Striptease* Alberto **1996**	*Boomtown* Officer Ray Hechler **2002–2003**
Mrs. Parker and the Vicious Circle Heywood Broun **1994**	*Unfaithful* Detective Mirojnick **2002**	

Clancy Brown

HEY! IT'S THAT
SCARY PSYCHO COP!

Stats:

VILLAIN

AS SEEN ON TV

PERIOD PIECE

STRAIGHT-TO-VIDEO

Clancy Brown may be the actor with the greatest degree of exposure on TV and the least crossover of his audiences.

The Shawshank Redemption's rebroadcast rights must have sold for about four dollars, because it's *always* on. In it, Brown plays Byron Hadley, the sadistic head screw at the titular prison. He dangles an inmate off a roof and looks the other way when another is beaten so badly he gets sent to a special prison for invalids. At the end, when Andy Dufresne (Tim Robbins) reveals the embezzlement he'd been hiding, the warden (corrupt in a supervisory capacity) shoots himself in the head; poor old Byron gets led off in handcuffs. Byron somehow didn't notice that white-collar bad guys find ways to beat the rap, whereas bad guys in uniforms go to jail.

None of that is appropriate viewing for children, of course, so Brown has widened his oeuvre to attract ankle-biters as well, voicing SpongeBob's boss Mr. Krabs, as well as dozens of other characters in cartoons and videogames. So if you're just passing by the den and hear that flat, steely voice wafting forth, you may not be able to tell, at first, whether it's in the service of a wholesome family show, like *SpongeBob*, or a creepy one, like *Carnivàle*. To our knowledge, that was never true of Mel Blanc.

The Bride	Starship Troopers	Carnivàle
Viktor the Monster	Career Sgt. Zim	Brother Justin Crowe
1985	**1997**	**2003—**

Highlander	ER
Victor Kruger/The Kurgan	Dr. Ellis West
1986	**1997–1998**

George Dzundza

HEY! IT'S THAT TRAGICALLY
DOOMED PARTNER
WHO'S JUST TWO WEEKS FROM RETIRING!

See George Dzundza? The cop at the end of the bar? That short, stumpy guy planted on the stool next to the handsome lady-killing detective? He's two weeks from retiring, that Dzundza is. All that hard work is finally paying off, with a gold watch and a handshake and a big, sloppy kiss goodbye.

He's telling his lady-killing partner to stay away from that woman. He's got a bad feeling about that one. Hell, he's got a bad feeling about this whole damn case. Besides which, he's too old for this shit. And he's just two weeks from retirement.

Which is why we hope he doesn't go into the abandoned warehouse. He should know better—just stay in the car! Call for back-up and wait it out! Or better yet, he should wile away his last two weeks pushing paper at some cushy desk job.

The Deer Hunter
John
1978

No Way Out
Sam Hesselman
1987

Crimson Tide
Chief of the Boat
1995

Salem's Lot
Cullen "Cully" Sawyer
1979

Law & Order
Sgt. Max Greevey
1990–1991

But his partner's in that warehouse, damn it! Or at least Dzundza thinks he is. He doesn't know it's all a trap—a setup! Well, he'll know soon enough, once he walks into the warehouse and finds it strangely empty and says, "Lady-killing partner? You in here?" and then notices the little red light on the little box on the wall. The one with the wires curling out of it.

And then the little red light turns green. Boom!

This has been George Dzundza's lot as an actor—to play the rumpled sidekick who's smart and wary and turns out to be right about everything, yet still gets blown up right before he's about to retire. And Michael Douglas (his lady-killing partner in **Basic Instinct**) gets to live, bed the hot chick, and, presumably, retire in peace. That, friends, is the definition of injustice.

HEY! IT'S CHAPTER TEN: THE PRECINCT

That Darn Cat
FBI Captain Boetticher
1997

Jesse
John Warner Sr.
1998–2000

Hack
Father Tom "Grizz" Grzelak
2002–2004

Species II
Col. Carter Burgess Jr.
1998

Instinct
Dr. John Murray
1999

Miguel Ferrer

Stats: MULTI-ETHNIC

HEY! IT'S THAT
UNSENTIMENTAL D.A.!

AS SEEN ON TV

Although Miguel Ferrer does look a bit like his dad, the dashing character actor José Ferrer, he doesn't look much like a guy whose name should be "Miguel Ferrer." (Nor, for that matter, does he look like his cousin, George Clooney—who could himself pass for a "Miguel Ferrer.")

Instead, Miguel Ferrer looks more like a guy whose name is "FBI Agent Albert Rosenfield." Or, if you squint, you might see a "Bob Morton"—the sniveling, ambitious sidekick from *RoboCop*. Or wait—take another gander and who do you see? That's right—"Chief Medical Examiner Garret Macy," Ferrer's role on the TV series *Crossing Jordan*.

Because Miguel Ferrer looks like a D.A. or a cop or a DEA agent or a medical examiner. On a good day, a Director of Hatcheries and Conditioning. (Yes, he played that role once, too.) Ferrer's career has been aided by the fact that he has just enough swarthy exoticism about him that, in Hollywood's mind, he can play any kind of foreigner, from Mr. Ortega Peru in *Mr. Magoo* to Tony Castellano in *Another Stakeout* to Stanislav in *A Promise Kept: The Oksana Baiul Story*.

We think he makes an especially good D.A. But we do hope that once, just once, he gets to wear a frilly white shirt and ravish a buxom maiden— just to make his dad, and his name, proud.

HEY! IT'S THAT GUY!

Star Trek III:
The Search for Spock
First Officer
1984

Twin Peaks
FBI Agent Albert Rosenfield
1990–1991

The Manchurian Candidate
Colonel Garret
2004

RoboCop
Bob Morton
1987

Brave New World
Director of Hatcheries
and Conditioning
1998

Paul Guilfoyle

Stats:

BALD

AWARD NOMINEE

THE...

MULTI-ETHNIC

AS SEEN ON TV

AS SEEN ON
TV

HEY! IT'S THAT
DEADPAN DETECTIVE!

Paul Guilfoyle's balding pate, unexceptional blancmange face, appraising squint, and condescending smirk have made him the ideal guest star on **Law & Order** (in the premiere episode, no less) and the actor of choice for red-herring corrupt cop roles in films like **The Negotiator**, **In Dreams**, and **Heaven's Prisoners**. Guilfoyle's nearly seventy major credits stretch all the way back to 1975—and not a significant leading role among them.

Guilfoyle's figure would seem to have pegged him as a low-on-the-totem-pole dirty cop until he landed the ultimate police role of his career: Captain Jim Brass on TV's drama series **CSI: Crime Scene Investigation**. While a recurring theme in the show has been the way the CSIs clash with upper police-force management, our forensic team has nothing to fear from Brass; he's a former CSI himself and is therefore wise enough to work closely with Gil Grissom, the chief investigator, and to heed his every bit of counsel. As well he should; the show has set Grissom up as a virtually infallible crime scene investigator of Columbo-esque proportions.

Jim Brass solves Las Vegas's seediest crimes, usually with some kind of gallows-humor pun as we smash into the opening credits. Why can't real cops be so quippy?

Wall Street Stone Livingston **1987**		*Air Force One* Chief of Staff Lloyd "Shep" Shepherd **1997**		*Anywhere But Here* George Franklin **1999**
	Quiz Show Lishman **1994**		*Primary Colors* Howard Ferguson **1998**	

Ted Levine

WIG/PROSTHESIS USE

ICONIC ROLE

VILLAIN

HEY! IT'S THAT
JITTERY PSYCHO
IN THE HOLDING CELL!

Ted Levine is best known for playing the serial killer Buffalo Bill in *The Silence of the Lambs*, which means he's famous for three things: 1) being the *other* bad guy in *The Silence of the Lambs*; 2) saying "It puts the lotion in the basket", and 3) dancing around naked in front of a mirror with his weenie tucked betwixt his thighs.

Otherwise, Levine is a good old-fashioned chameleon. Throw some scruff on him and you've got a petty thief; give him a buzzcut (or, more specifically, a buzzcut-esque hairpiece) and you've got an astronaut hero; trim those locks and temper that jitteriness and you've got Capt. Leland Stottlemeyer, the perpetually aggravated boss to Tony Shalhoub on TV's *Monk*.

It's quite possible that the very attribute—a kind of anonymous malleability—that's brought Levine such success as a character actor will prevent him from breaking out in the manner of, say, Gary Sinise or William H. Macy. For example, he was in *Heat*, *Ali*, and *Wild Wild West* and very good in each. But can you remember him? At all?

That said, he may yet break through, perhaps thanks to a memorable turn in a popular hit. Until that day, enjoy him. If you can find him, that is.

HEY! IT'S THAT GUY!

162

Flubber	The Fast and the Furious	The Manchurian Candidate
Wesson	Sgt. Tanner	Colonel Howard
1997	**2001**	**2004**

Moby Dick	Monk
Starbuck	Capt. Leland Stottlemeyer
1998	**2002**

Bill Nunn

Stats: | ICONIC ROLE

HEY! IT'S THAT TOWERING RIGHTEOUS **DETECTIVE!**

Do you love Bill Nunn, or hate him? Love or hate? Love! Hate! Love! Hate!

For our part, we love him. Especially when he's thrusting those big, bejeweled fists in our faces.

We're referring, of course, to his seminal role as Radio Raheem in 1989's *Do the Right Thing*—you know, the guy who carried the huge radio and had LOVE and HATE written on two large rings across the knuckles of his hands. That role set the tone for Nunn's career, which he's largely spent playing . . . well, large men: often intimidating, always imposing.

Surprisingly, though, Nunn doesn't play many thugs or villains, perhaps because he's so big and intimidating that, if he did, the cop movies would all have to have titles like *Retreat* and *Mad Scramble for the Exit* and *Did You See the Size of That Guy?* and *I Wet My Pants in San Francisco*.

Also, Nunn has a soft side—that kind of huge-guy teddy-bear syndrome—that makes him a welcome presence in any movie. We'd certainly like to see more of him, just as Linda Fiorentino did in *The Last Seduction*, when he showed her his manhood. Though we promise not to kill him right after, like she did. Yeah, like we even could. We'd have LOVE and HATE embedded in our foreheads for life.

Sister Act	*Kiss the Girls*	*Runaway Jury*
Lt. Eddie Souther	Det. John Sampson	Lonnie Shaver
1992	**1997**	**2003**

The Last Seduction	*Spider-Man/Spider-Man 2*
Harlan	Joseph "Robbie" Robertson
1994	**2002/2004**

Jon Polito

HEY! IT'S THAT
ROTUND SNITCH!

Jon Polito just wasn't made for these times.

There used to be an era, back in the days of *The Maltese Falcon*, *Casablanca*, and Peter Lorre in *M*, when Hollywood valued the weasel, the slippery rat, and the rotund double-crosser. Unfortunately for Jon Polito, those times are not these times, and we're all the poorer for it.

If you need proof, just look at what happened to him in 1994. Polito, an actor who, with his spherical stature and shifty, sweaty demeanor, often comes across as a snowman made of Crisco, had finally procured a feature role on a smart new TV series: that of Detective Steve Crossetti on the critically lauded ***Homicide: Life on the Street***. This was good news for fans of Polito's memorable turns in ***Barton Fink*** (as sniveling movie producer Lou Breeze) and ***Miller's Crossing*** (as sputtering gangster Johnny "You're giving me the high hat!" Caspar). Pre-*Homicide*, Polito had established himself as an art-house Joe Pesci, a thinking man's Danny DeVito. Now, it

Miller's Crossing
Johnny Caspar
1990

The Rocketeer
Otis Bigelow,
Airfield Owner
1991

The Hudsucker Proxy
Mr. Bumstead
1994

Barton Fink
Lou Breeze
1991

Homicide:
Life on the Street
Det. Steve Crosetti
1993–1994

seemed, he'd have a weekly national platform from which we could all indulge in his particular talents.

But *Homicide*'s ratings flatlined, and in an effort to improve them, the producers tossed out many of the compelling character actors and trucked in more photogenic, less interesting replacements. Out went Polito, in came the hunky Reed Diamond, and, to our mind, the show was never quite the same.

Not that Polito hasn't found work since: The year 2001 alone found him in no fewer than six films. Hollywood will always have room for double-crossers, cheats, slimeballs, and liars—not to mention actors who can play those parts well. But with his darting eyes and needle-thin mustache, Jon Polito will always seem like a throwback to another era, when the sweaty of brow and shifty of eye were just as valued as the square of jaw and sparkly of smile.

The Crow
Gideon,
the Pawn Shop Owner
1994

*The Adventures of
Rocky & Bullwinkle*
Schoentell
2000

The Man Who Wasn't There
Creighton Tolliver
2001

The Big Lebowski
Da Fino
1998

The Tailor of Panama
Ramon Rudd
2001

View from the Top
Roy Roby
2003

C. C. H. Pounder

**HEY! IT'S THAT
STEELY AND UNFLAPPABLE
LADY COP!**

A few relevant details about C. C. H. Pounder:

Pounder is an actress, not a late '80s dance group. (That's C&C Music Factory.) Pounder has, however, put out an album and can sing, quite well, as evidenced in the film ***Bagdad Café***. (Her album, by most accounts, was not as successful; one review called it "flat, rhythmless, bad-funny.") Pounder was born in Guyana. The "C. C. H." in "C. C. H. Pounder" stands for "Carol Christine Hilaria," which, to our knowledge, makes her the most famous person with the name "Hilaria" in all of human history.

You may recognize Pounder from her three-year stint as Dr. Angela Hicks on ***ER***, or you may recognize her as the steely and unflappable cop, Claudette Wyms, from FX's ***The Shield***. Heck, you may even recognize her from ***RoboCop 3***—who are we to judge?

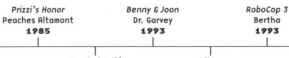

Prizzi's Honor	Benny & Joon	RoboCop 3
Peaches Altamont	Dr. Garvey	Bertha
1985	**1993**	**1993**

Bagdad Café	Sliver
Brenda	Lt. Victoria Hendrix
1988	**1993**

But Pounder's substantial résumé runs back to 1979 and, at last count, was more than 65 roles deep, most of which start with "Detective" or "Lieutenant" or "Nurse" or "Doctor." Pounder's become a sort of living embodiment of Hollywood's continued efforts to promote gender and racial diversity in its own fictional police stations and hospitals, if only in the background, behind the white people.

And because she's been so good, she's probably responsible, more than anyone, for the fact that the steely and determined black lady cop is now a staple character on primetime cop shows—shows like *Law & Order* (featuring the serious S. Epatha Merkerson) and *Without a Trace* (featuring the steely Marianne Jean-Baptiste). That alone is a testament to Pounder's considerable talents. That she also put out all those great dance hits in the '80s is just a bonus.

ER
Dr. Angela Hicks
1994–1997

Face/Off
Dr. Hollis Miller
1997

End of Days
Det. Margie Francis
1999

The Shield
Claudette Wyms
2002–

It's the first day of school; the coming year could bring all kinds of triumphs and traumas. There's the bell! Better get to class, where you may find kind class-mates who'll make friends with you, gigantic bullies who'll steal your lunch money, or tough girls who'll try to trick you into getting them pregnant. Your homeroom teacher could be a sweet-natured professional who'll mentor you toward admission to a good college (for example, convincing that hard-assed

HEY! IT'S CHAPTER ELEVEN:
THE SCHOOL

coach to give you a shot on the basketball team), or he could be a tenured jack-ass who takes no greater pleasure in life than in tormenting his students. Better not be late, or you'll get sent to the principal's office, which may be occupied by a single-minded sadist or merely an ineffectual figurehead. And be careful that you don't accidentally leave a wadded-up note or a half-finished milk carton on the floor in the hall: You do *not* want to get on the janitor's bad side.

Troy Evans

HEY! IT'S THAT DOOFUS
SPORTS COACH
WITH A BUZZCUT!

We can imagine quite easily a short film in which Troy Evans, perhaps best known as the coach from *Teen Wolf*, plays virtually every part.

Imagine the scene: a small-town police station. Desk Sergeant Troy Evans stands idly reading a newspaper. Troy Evans, the local high school basketball coach, bursts through the door.

COACH EVANS: Sarge, someone's stolen all of our uniforms! And tonight's the big game against State!

SERGEANT EVANS: Hold on there, Coach. Let me call the sheriff.

SHERIFF EVANS: Say there, Coach, shouldn't you be down at the high school getting ready for the big game against State? And I hope that teen werewolf is ready to play!

COACH EVANS: That's what I was trying to tell the sarge. All our uniforms are missing! And the teen wolfboy is ready, but now he's decided he doesn't want to play as the wolf anymore! He just wants to play as a human boy. But he's sure not going to play naked—none of my boys will!

From there, we're whisked to the big game, where it turns out that Troy Evans, an evil Army general, stole all the uniforms because his son wasn't getting playing time, thanks to that hell-spawn wolfboy. Luckily, in walks Michael Jordan (as himself), who leads the team to victory. Roll credits.

Twin Peaks	*Ace Ventura: Pet Detective*	*ER*
Principal George Wolchezk	Roger Podacter	Frank Martin
1990	**1994**	**2000–**
	Demolition Man	*Fear and Loathing in Las Vegas*
	Tough Cop	Police Chief
	1993	**1998**

Paul Gleason

HEY! IT'S THAT HEARTLESS
AUTHORITARIAN JERK!

Stats: ICONIC ROLE

VILLAIN

Extend the index and pinkie fingers of your hand, to make what is sometimes referred to as the "rock on" hand. This is "the bull." Now spin your hand around so that the palm is facing you. These are "the horns." And if you know anything about Paul Gleason, you know that if you mess with one, you'll get the other.

Until 1985, Paul Gleason played lots of typical H!ITG! roles: lieutenants and sergeants and police detectives. Then Gleason landed the role that would brand him on the brains of every '80s-era teenager: Principal Richard Vernon, the preening warden to five imprisoned kids in *The Breakfast Club*. For most character actors, one performance this monumental would be enough in a career. Gleason, however, added another nearly-as-iconic role to his résumé: the preening FBI Deputy Police Chief Dwayne T. Robinson in *Die Hard*.

How iconic were these roles? Well, Gleason spoofed both of them later in his career, reviving Richard Vernon in the teen comedy *Not Another Teen Movie* and playing FBI Agent Dwayne T. Robinson in the action spoof *Loaded Weapon*. So we'd like to extend our index finger and pinkie in a salute to Paul Gleason. Though this time, we aren't making the bull. This is the "rock on" hand.

The Great Santini
Lt. Sammy
1979

Trading Places
Clarence Beeks
1983

Miami Blues
Sgt. Frank Lackley
1990

Arthur
Executive
1981

Die Hard
Deputy Police Chief
Dwayne T. Robinson
1988

Jeffrey Jones

HEY! IT'S THAT
SNEERING, SLIGHTLY UNHINGED
DEAN OF STUDENTS!

Jeffrey Jones and the late, great J. T. Walsh (page 102) seem to have little in common—other than their incredibly long résumés. Jones is best remembered by all of us as the resourceful yet ultimately bested and finally hysterical dean of students on a rampage, Ed Rooney, of *Ferris Bueller's Day Off*. Walsh played many a bested character in his time, but even in defeat, Walsh was always able to maintain the steely composure of a man who could still crush your larynx. Think of Jeffrey Jones in the last half-hour of *Bueller*. Can you picture J. T. Walsh ever sinking up to his ankle in a mud puddle? Getting kicked in the face by a female high-school sophomore? *Riding on a school bus?* The very idea is ludicrous.

    Jeffrey Jones is the only character actor of Walsh's caliber working today, and he actually has one significant advantage over the late Walsh

Amadeus
Emperor Joseph II
1984

Beetlejuice
Charles
1988

Ferris Bueller's Day Off
Ed Rooney
1986

Stay Tuned
Spike
1992

(other than, you know, life itself): Jeffrey Jones is like J. T. Walsh if Walsh had the capacity to feel and express joy.

Jeffrey Jones wears powdered wigs (*Amadeus*, *Valmont*, *The Crucible*, *Sleepy Hollow*). He does comedy—the broader (*Houseguest*, *Stay Tuned*, *Heartbreakers*), the better. He appears opposite CG animals (*Stuart Little*, *Dr. Dolittle 2*), zombies (*Beetlejuice*), and John Leguizamo (*The Pest*). He's every bit as prolific as Walsh ever was; the difference is that Jones sometimes seems to be having fun.

We all have to come to terms with the fact that there was only one J. T. Walsh. We'll never have another. We were lucky to have him at all. And we should be grateful that, now that Walsh has left us, we still have Jeffrey Jones.

Ed Wood
Criswell
1994

Ravenous
Col. Hart
1999

The Crucible
Thomas Putnam
1996

Deadwood
A. W. Merrick
2004–

John Kapelos

CANADIAN

ICONIC ROLE

BALD

AS SEEN ON TV

HEY! IT'S THAT
ALL-SEEING JANITOR!

Among other lessons, the kids in *The Breakfast Club* learned that, thanks to just a few wrong moves in life, they might end up stuck in a high school . . . *for the rest of their lives.* This lesson was learned from Carl the Janitor, played by Mr. John Kapelos.

Carl the Janitor doesn't get a lot of screen time, but he imparts a wealth of wisdom. Carl the Janitor had dreams once, but he isn't taken seriously now. However, *Carl the Janitor sees all.* Bender (Judd Nelson) tries to score some easy points with his fellow delinquents by making fun of Carl, but Carl responds by shooting back a monologue to the effect that nothing happens in the school that he, in the course of his janitorial rounds, doesn't know about. Thus Carl the Janitor earns Bender's grudging respect.

Kapelos has played more than a hundred other roles, ranging from *Late Show with David Letterman* producer Robert Morton in the HBO movie *The Late Shift* to Canadian TV star Bruno Gerussi in the Bob Crane biopic *Auto Focus.* But none has been as indelible as his wise and world-weary Chicago-area maintenance engineer, Carl the Janitor. Don't sass him, or he'll clean your mouth out and steal the weed from your locker.

HEY! IT'S THAT GUY!

Sixteen Candles
Rudy Ryszczyk
1984

Off Beat
Lou Wareham
1986

Forever Knight
Det. Don Schanke
1992–1995

Weird Science
Dino
1992

Roxanne
Chuck
1987

Taryn Manning

Stats: | DOUBLE THREAT

HEY! IT'S THAT
TRASHY FRIEND!

From Desdemona's Emilia to Sandy's Rizzo, the Trashy Friend helps the Good Girl attempt skankiness by teaching her how to smoke or giving her a slutty makeover. Since no Good Girl ever truly turns trashy, the Trashy Friend also throws the Good Girl's goodness into sharp relief.

In **Crossroads**, Britney Spears's Lucy is high school valedictorian, med-school bound, and a virgin. Taryn Manning is Mimi, the class outcast, a skanky dresser, and scandalously *pregnant*. Mimi loses her baby and is redeemed from her trashiness by her friendship with Good Girl Lucy.

In **crazy/beautiful**, emotionally unstable Nicole (Kirsten Dunst) is trashy, but to merit the love of sensible Carlos (Jay Hernandez), she must shed Even Trashier Friends, including Manning's Maddy, so craggy she looks closer to age 30 than age 18.

Niki, a corrupt foster child Manning played in **White Oleander**, is the last straw for Astrid; soon Astrid will decide to get her life back on track. Niki mostly serves just as another interchangeable element of trashiness in Astrid's foster nightmare.

Manning went on to play Janeane, Brittany Murphy's Even Trashier Friend in **8 Mile**. Only Manning herself can say whether she felt cheaper plying her craft in the service of Spears or Eminem. At least Britney probably never tried to make Manning give her a blowjob.

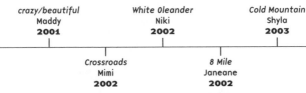

crazy/beautiful	White Oleander	Cold Mountain
Maddy	Niki	Shyla
2001	**2002**	**2003**

Crossroads	8 Mile
Mimi	Janeane
2002	**2002**

Edie McClurg

HEY! IT'S THAT ANNOYING, BUSYBODY **SECRETARY!**

You know Edie McClurg, even if you don't know you know her. To a certain generation, she'll always be Herb Tarlek's annoying, busybody wife, Lucille, from **WKRP in Cincinnati**. To another generation, she's Dean of Students Rooney's annoying, busybody secretary in **Ferris Bueller's Day Off**. To another generation, she's the annoying, busybody campus tour guide in National Lampoon's **Van Wilder**, though that generation really needs to get out to the video store and rent Ferris Bueller's Day Off.

She's graced everything from forgotten '80s-era sitcoms such as **Small Wonder** (in which she played an annoying, busybody neighbor) to **The Hogan Family** (in which she played an annoying, busybody neighbor) to **Dickie Roberts: Former Child Star** (in which she played an annoying, busybody neighbor). In fact, she's played so many annoying, busybody neighbors that you might ask, "Why is her habitat the school? Why not the suburbs?" Well, eventually the annoying, busybody secretary has to go home and be somebody's neighbor.

Edie McClurg, though, is such a good, useful H!ITG! that she's become a kind of uber-H!ITG! For example, she now only needs to show up onscreen for a second and you automatically register "annoying busybody." She has honed her H!ITG! powers to peak efficiency.

The Pee-Wee Herman Show Hermit Hattie **1981**		Planes, Trains & Automobiles Car Rental Agent **1987**		Flubber Martha George **1997**
	Mr. Mom Checkout Lady **1983**		Natural Born Killers Mallory's Mom **1994**	

Lochlyn Munro

HEY! IT'S THAT FRATBOY
CHUCKLEHEAD!

Stats: CANADIAN

VILLAIN

AS SEEN ON TV

Lochlyn Munro is the King of the Chuckleheads. It's ironic that he has such a lyrical name given that so many of his characters have names like Larry, Billy, Craig, Scott, Eddie, and Ted.

Back in his younger years, he was well-known as the tough-but-tender heartthrob on **Northwood**, a Canadian high school drama not entirely unlike its more internationally famous cousin, *Degrassi Junior High*. So Canadians always get a charge seeing him in films such as **Dracula 2000**, **Screwed**, **A Night at the Roxbury**, **Dead Man on Campus**, or **A Guy Thing**. He also pops up in a lot of TV movies, such as **Abduction of Innocence** or the best-titled TV movie of all time, **Mother, May I Sleep with Danger?** In that movie, he even got a last name: Kevin Shane. Although that's really just two chucklehead first names strung together.

Let's face it: With his thick neck and cherubic mug, he makes the perfect jock slash obnoxious fratboy. But now that he's growing older, he may have to leave the fratboy roles behind. Take, for example, **Freddy Vs. Jason**, in which he plays Deputy Scott. The fratboy got a job!

Northwood		*Scary Movie*		*White Chicks*
Jason		Greg Phillippe		Agent Jake Harper
1991–1993		**2000**		**2004**
	Unforgiven		*Duets*	
	Texas Slim		Ronny Jackson	
	1992		**2000**	

Vincent Schiavelli

Stats: **HALL OF FAME**

HEY! IT'S THAT FREAKY-LOOKING
SCIENCE TEACHER!

MULTI-ETHNIC

BALD

AS SEEN ON TV

Your average Hey! It's That Guy! is, well, average looking, blending easily from role to role. He is Hollywood wallpaper. Vincent Schiavelli is *not* wallpaper. He is freaky looking. He's not blending easily into anything, except maybe your night-mares. See him once, and he catches your eye. See him again, and he catches your eye, puts it in a cage, gives it a name, and keeps it as a pet. We don't want to say what happens when you see him a third time.

Chances are, you've seen him plenty of times already, whether as the freaky-looking alien villain in *Buckaroo Banzai* or the freaky-looking spook in *Ghost* or the freaky-looking teachers in *Fast Times at Ridgemont High* and *Better Off Dead*.

In fact, wherever freaky-looking people are needed—whether in hippie communes, behind the wheels of taxicabs, in mental asylums, in high school teachers' lounges, or in hell—Vincent Schiavelli will be there. He's the Tom Joad of freaky looking.

Enjoy him. Relish him. And don't let his looks distract you from one very simple, very obvious fact: Schiavelli is a very fine actor, with a very fine career, who's made every movie he's been in just a little bit better. He just happens to be a very fine actor who's also six-foot-five, with crazy, mad-scientist hair and a face as long and thin as a windsock.

Amadeus	*The People vs. Larry Flynt*	*Death to Smoochy*
Salieri's Valet	Chester	Buggy Ding Dong
1984	**1996**	**2002**

Better Off Dead	*Man on the Moon*
Mr. Kerber	Maynard Smith
1985	**1999**

Wallace Shawn

Stats:

DOUBLE-THREAT

2.

HALL OF FAME

⭐

HEY! IT'S THAT STUDENT-SPRITZING
ENGLISH TEACHER
WITH A SECRET!

Wallace Shawn, the movie actor, is a straight-down-the-middle character type: the buggy eyes, the fishy lips, the "Thuffering Thuccotash!" thibilant lisp. He's best known to most people over the age of 30 as the "Inconthceivable!" guy from **The Princess Bride**. He's best known to people under 30 as the sweet, student-spritzing teacher from **Clueless**.

But Wallace Shawn, the man, is far more interesting. He is an award-winning playwright. He is the son of *The New Yorker*'s former editor, the famously eccentric William Shawn. He's part of a Manhattan demimonde of artsy intelligentsia that feels straight out of a Woody Allen movie, largely because it includes Woody Allen.

Did we mention he also played the teacher in *Clueless*?

Wallace Shawn is one of a very few actors who are actually far more interesting in real life than are any of their onscreen characters. That's the beauty of a double threat like Shawn. He's like a cereal box with an unexpected toy inside. With Shawn, the more you learn about him, the more interesting he becomes. It's like finding out your high school guidance counselor is also a world-class salsa dancer. And how many other movie stars can you say that about?

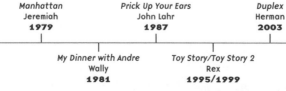

Manhattan Jeremiah **1979**	*Prick Up Your Ears* John Lahr **1987**	*Duplex* Herman **2003**
My Dinner with Andre Wally **1981**	*Toy Story/Toy Story 2* Rex **1995/1999**	

Gedde Watanabe

HEY! IT'S THAT
EXCHANGE STUDENT!

FOREIGNER

STRAIGHT-TO-VIDEO

It probably seemed like a good career move at the time. Here was a chance for an unknown actor to play a lead role in a big teen comedy. Okay, so the "character" was an exchange student named Long Duk Dong, whose big moments consisted of drunkenly falling out of a tree kamikaze-style (those crazy Asians!) and dancing with a large-bosomed woman with his head planted deep in her cleavage (those really short Asians!).

Yes, this was the foot in the door. This would lead to bigger things. Only it didn't. Gedde Watanabe is a fine, funny actor who most everyone, to this day, remembers as Long Duk Dong, the exchange student from **Sixteen Candles**. Recently, his situation has been looking up. Fans of **ER** have enjoyed him in the role of Nurse Yosh Takata.

Those encouraged by these developments, however, may be dismayed to learn that, in the 1998 disaster film **Armageddon**, he appeared as a character named, simply, "Asian Tourist." Then, in the 2002 teen comedy **Slackers**, he played "Japanese Proctor." At least in *Sixteen Candles* he got to have a name, even if it was a joke about a waterfowl's penis.

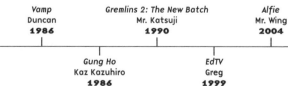

Vamp
Duncan
1986

Gremlins 2: The New Batch
Mr. Katsuji
1990

Alfie
Mr. Wing
2004

Gung Ho
Kaz Kazuhiro
1986

EdTV
Greg
1999

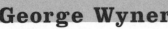

George Wyner

HEY! IT'S THAT
COMICALLY INEFFECTUAL
PRINCIPAL!

Stats: BALD

AS SEEN ON TV

George Wyner has oversized glasses, a gawky manner, a balding pate, and puckered lips—pursed as though in a perpetual grimace of dismay and distaste. He's been a go-to geek in Hollywood for more than three decades. His résumé, in fact, is a primer in Hollywood's nomenclature of the nebbish, featuring such character names as Myron Fein, Ratkowski, Dr. Irving Lefkowitz, Dr. Fishbeck, Mr. Cornish, Saul Panzer, and Meisel.

Wyner's been ineffectual—purposefully ineffectual, effectively ineffectual, comically ineffectual—in such films as *The Postman*, *The Devil's Advocate*, *Spaceballs*, *Fletch*, and *Fletch Lives*. He makes an especially effective ineffectual school principal, as he proved in both *Wildcats* and *Not Another Teen Movie*. And he served a two-year stint as the comically ineffectual Deputy Max Rubin on the uncomical, inadvertently ineffectual Suzanne Somers vehicle, *She's the Sheriff*.

Aside from their prodigious ineffectuality, Wyner's characters have one other thing in common: They are losers. And not just any losers, but unlovable, butt-of-the-joke losers. Of course, to have jokes, there have to be butts of jokes. And among the butts, Wyner's been one of the best.

The Bad News Bears White Sox Manager **1976**		*Spaceballs* Colonel Sandurz **1987**		*American Pie 2* Camp Director **2001**
	Wildcats Principal Walker **1986**		*The Devil's Advocate* Meisel **1997**	

Given that Hollywood movies and TV shows are, you know, *made* in studios, you'd think that the fictional studio types would be portrayed in a flattering light: philanthropic studio heads, kindly floor directors, hardworking on-air talent, well-spoken and thoughtful agents. But you know what? Not so much. We don't know if it's a sign of Hollywood self-loathing, or a healthy sense of self-deprecation, or internecine backstabbing (writers write evil directors, directors

THE STUDIO

craft horrible actors, actors play baleful writers—and everyone hates agents), or, simply, a bracing and uncharacteristic truthfulness. But for whatever reason, nearly every creature you find in the studio is loathsome, irritating, unctuous, insincere, or all of the above. And dumb. A lot of them are just plain dumb. All the people in Hollywood can't be this bad, can they? Except the agents, of course. We suspect that the agents are, in fact, this bad.

William Atherton

Stats:

VILLAIN

PERIOD PIECE

AS SEEN ON TV

HEY! IT'S THAT POMPOUS
TWIT TV REPORTER!

First off, we apologize, William Atherton, for calling you a pompous twit. But come on—you do it so well! You're the number-one nincompoop, the dean of donkey's asses. You used your extraordinary talent for unctuousness to create not one but two iconic roles: Walter Peck, the prissy EPA lawyer in *Ghostbusters*, and Richard Thornburg, the sleazy TV reporter in *Die Hard* and *Die Hard 2*.

Even their names are grating: *Walter Peck* and *Richard Thornburg*. We already want to slap you! Or punch you in your smug kisser, just like Bonnie Bedelia did at the end of *Die Hard*. You endangered her man, and for what? A lousy scoop! TV reporters—aargghhh! They're the worst!

And Walter Peck—well, there, you took the cake. Can't you see these ghostbusters have ghosts to bust? Stop getting in the way before you accidentally loose evil spirits all over the—oops, you just did.

That said, we thank you, William Atherton. We thank you because you help to uphold Hollywood's moral code. In that code, pompous twits always get their comeuppance—whether it's a punch in the face or a dousing in ectoplasmic goo. And you've always taken that comeuppance and bounced back like a man—a grating, pompous, irritating man.

Real Genius Prof. Jerry Hathaway **1985**	*Bio-Dome* Dr. Noah Faulkner **1996**	*The Last Samurai* Winchester Rep **2003**
The Pelican Brief Bob Gminski **1993**	*Mad City* Dohlen **1997**	

Bob Balaban

HEY! IT'S THAT
SARDONIC, NEBBISHY
NETWORK EXECUTIVE!

AS SEEN ON TV

BALD

AWARD NOMINEE

Ever since Woody Allen turned the sputtering, neurotic nebbish into an American archetype, Hollywood has been awash in sputtering, neurotic nebbishes. And this is why Bob Balaban is very smart. Rather than climb aboard the overcrowded Woody Allen Manqué Express, he recognized and exploited a previously unfilled nebbish niche: the soft-spoken, occasionally sardonic nebbish.

As evidenced in his signature turns in the '90s as the head of NBC (which he's played in two different forms: once, as the Warren Littlefield clone Russell Dalrymple on **Seinfeld**, and later, as the actual Warren Littlefield in **The Late Shift**), Balaban has perfected a delivery that is, paradoxically, equal parts droll defeat and deadpan disdain.

Balaban's talent for dreary deadpan—he's like a hyper-intelligent version of the old Hanna Barbera cartoon character Droopy Dog—have since been on display in **Waiting for Guffman** (as long-suffering music teacher Lloyd Miller), **Clockwatchers** (as corporate drone Milton Lasky), and **Best in Show** (as exquisitely named dog expert Dr. Theodore W. Millbank III). And, as if you needed one more reason to like and admire Bob Balaban, try saying "Bob Balaban" several times as quickly as you can. It will make your lips feel nice.

Waiting for Guffman Lloyd Miller **1996**	*Ghost World* Enid's Dad **2000**	*A Mighty Wind* Jonathan Steinbloom **2003**
	Deconstructing Harry Richard **1997**	*Gosford Park* Morris Weissman **2001**

Seymour Cassel

HEY! IT'S THAT OUT-OF-TOUCH
TALENT AGENT!

In the late '60s and the '70s, Seymour Cassel was in the vanguard of independent film actors, making half a dozen pictures with writer/director John Cassavetes. He was even Oscar nominated for his performance in Cassavetes's *Faces*. And yet, these achievements are unknown to a generation that last saw him as Morty O'Reilly, the grinning, rundown talent agent to a pair of conjoined twins in *Stuck on You*.

And, uh . . . *we* are in that generation.

Fortunately for us, Seymour Cassel has had a career resurgence, starting in the late '90s. Even though he turns up in some stinkers—like *Stealing Harvard* and *The Crew*—he makes good movies, too. You may have picked him out of the virtual sea of Hey! It's That Guy!s populating the earnest, baseball-themed period drama *61**, for instance, in the service of another Cassavetes-like actor/auteur: Mr. Billy Crystal.

Cassel has, in his twilight years, hooked up with another generation-defining director: Wes Anderson. Cassel's gentle, shambling persona meshes

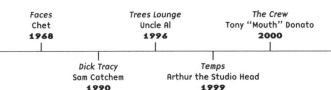

Faces Chet **1968**		*Trees Lounge* Uncle Al **1996**		*The Crew* Tony "Mouth" Donato **2000**
	Dick Tracy Sam Catchem **1990**		*Temps* Arthur the Studio Head **1999**	

beautifully with the tone of Anderson's sweet-yet-darkly-comic cinematic fables. In **The Royal Tenenbaums**, Cassel is Dusty, a courtly hotel doorman who's not above posing as a doctor to help pal Royal Tenenbaum (Gene Hackman) in his crooked scheme to get back together with his wife (Angelica Houston) by pretending to be dying of cancer; Dusty takes to the role so well that he's diagnosing an eye injury by the end of the film.

But our favorite Cassel role by a mile is Bert Fischer in **Rushmore**. Bert may be faintly befuddled by his exceptional-if-academically-challenged son, Max (Jason Schwartzman), but he's unquestioningly supportive of everything he does. He may have some idea that Max is ashamed of his modest station in life as a barber, but it doesn't seem to faze him.

Cassel has also played an extraordinary number of gangsters. But we prefer to think of him playing nice men: confused old agents speeding along the streets of L.A. on their Rascals and old-school barbers who still oil their hair.

61*
Sam Simon
2001

The Biz
Eugene Hinkle
2002

Stuck on You
Morty O'Reilly
2003

The Burial Society
Sam Goldberg
2002

Lucky
The Trake
2003

Judah Friedlander

AWARD NOMINEE

NEW SCHOOL

DISTINCTIVE FACIAL HAIR

HEY! IT'S THAT
DOPEY CAMERAMAN!

Judah Friedlander has impressive range playing simpletons, from high-functioning boobs (like Techie on the short-lived sit-com *Lateline* and Julio, the cameraman in *Showtime*) to actually mentally challenged persons (sunscreen-enthusiast-cum-card-trick-solver Donald on *Curb Your Enthusiasm*) to your garden-variety idiots who exist somewhere in between (Molly Shannon's ex, Ron, in *Wet Hot American Summer*). Friedlander is so good playing dimwits that he even infused comedy into the mute role of Derek's coal-mining brother Scrappy in *Zoolander*. It takes a particular kind of actor to keep his dignity while spending his time onscreen in a Cosby sweater, his mouth perpetually hanging half-open in a drooling stupor.

In 2003, Friedlander switched it up with a new twist on his standard role. As Toby Radloff in *American Splendor*, Friendlander had the challenge of playing not only a real person, but one who would appear—as himself—in the same film. It's a testament to how singular a character Toby is that he makes his best friend Harvey Pekar (Paul Giamatti, page 144) look like a real smooth smoothie. Even if he didn't shave every day and could probably do with having his adenoids removed.

Lateline
Techie
1998–1999

Zoolander
Scrappy Zoolander
2001

American Splendor
Toby Radloff
2003

Wet Hot American Summer
Ron
2001

Showtime
Julio
2002

Harriet Sansom Harris

**HEY! IT'S THAT
CONSCIENCELESS
AGENT!**

ICONIC ROLE

Harriet Sansom Harris is a supremely cool middle-aged woman with the throaty purr of an old-time noir vixen and the face of a cartoon squirrel. Two Harris roles we particularly enjoy:

1. Agent Bebe Glazer on *Frasier*. It was often the case on *Frasier* that the funniest characters were the ones who really pissed off the show's insufferable blowhard of a title character. Bebe—gleefully amoral and venal—is batshit crazy in the most entertaining way. She's seemingly unhinged but ultimately in complete control, of herself and most every situation.

2. Ellen in *Nurse Betty*. Ellen is a waitress in a bar at which Betty stops on her way to Los Angeles. Ellen's attitude toward the deeply confused Betty is not that different from the audience's: a mixture of impatience and indulgence, as one regards a person who is annoying but endearing. Harris infuses Ellen with that kind of world-weary, seen-it-all, impersonal warmth that lifelong waitresses often exhibit. Ellen gets additional cool points for being the only person who doesn't buy Morgan Freeman's character's cover story and also for the bad-ass Bonnie Raitt skunk streak in her hair.

Harriet Sansom Harris is a cool lady. She deserves every last nut she can sock away for winter in her hollowed-out cartoon tree.

Quiz Show Enright's Secretary **1994**	*Stark Raving Mad* Audrey **1999–2000**	*It's All Relative* Audrey O'Neil **2003–2004**
	Romeo + Juliet Susan Santandiago **1996**	*Memento* Mrs. Jankis **2000**

Christopher McDonald

Stats: AS SEEN ON TV

**HEY! IT'S THAT SMARMY
WEATHERMAN/CHEESY
GAME-SHOW HOST!**

VILLAIN

Some actors are blessed with charm; Christopher McDonald is blessed with smarm. He possesses a pure, old-school smarm: two parts country club, one part used-car salesman, and one part Caesar's Palace. We prefer this brew to new-jack smarm, which is exemplified in the person of Craig Kilborn: two parts fratboy, one part Wall Street, one part *Harvard Lampoon* "Poonie."

While charm is handy for leading men and politicians, smarm is a much more useful attribute for character actors. Smarm's very versatile. Buff it to a high gloss, and you can play the TV weatherman in ***The Perfect Storm***, the quiz-show host in ***Quiz Show***, or the self-help shill Tappy Tibbons in ***Requiem for a Dream***. Add a little malevolence, and you make a perfect snobby jerk, such as Shooter McGavin in ***Happy Gilmore***. Take the malevolent smarm downmarket and you've got Darryl, the redneck husband in ***Thelma & Louise***. Now strain the smarm and reduce over a low heat, stir in banality, and presto! You've got Ward Cleaver in the 1997 ***Leave It to Beaver*** remake.

No one's ever been able to bring the smarm quite like our man McDonald. He is to smarm what FedEx is to packages, what Roger Clemens is to fastballs, what FTD is to flowers in mugs: special delivery.

Grease 2	*Grumpy Old Men*	*The Man Who Wasn't There*
Goose McKenzie	Mike	Macadam Salesman
1982	**1993**	**2001**

Thelma & Louise	*61★*
Darryl	Mel Allen
1991	**2001**

Larry Miller

Stats: **BALD**

POSSE MEMBER

AS SEEN ON TV

HEY! IT'S THAT
SMILING BUFFOON!

Quiet, please, as we approach the natural habitat of the smiling buffoon. Please don't startle him. You'll notice he's quite jumpy. You'll also observe that no matter what he encounters, his face almost always remains frozen in a mask of insincere joy.

Please understand that this particular specimen, Larry Miller, was raised in captivity, on a stand-up comedy stage. So he's quite an accomplished comedian and very adept at aping the behavior of buffoons around him, be they principals, university deans, office bosses, or (especially) Hollywood agents. He's especially wondrous to behold when he travels with the herd led by Christopher Guest, who belongs to the rare and resplendent species known as *comedia mockumentaris*.

If you close your eyes, you can hear the buffoon's mating call. His mating call is a matter of some zoological confusion: He's not successful with the ladies, yet he seems to mate often, given that there are smiling buffoons everywhere. It is a species that, sadly, is not even close to extinction.

Also, the buffoon is a close cousin to the baboon, in that a baboon has a face and a big, round, red ass, while the smiling buffoon is a big, round, red-faced ass. So you can see the similarities.

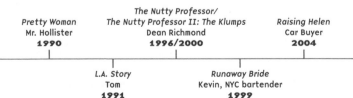

		The Nutty Professor/		
Pretty Woman		*The Nutty Professor II: The Klumps*		*Raising Helen*
Mr. Hollister		Dean Richmond		Car Buyer
1990		**1996/2000**		**2004**
	L.A. Story		*Runaway Bride*	
	Tom		Kevin, NYC bartender	
	1991		**1999**	

David Paymer

HEY! IT'S THAT
FAST-TALKING SHARK!

David Paymer generally looks so unassuming that it is delightful when he gets to bust out in a juicy role as a showbiz producer. Paymer plays other kinds of entertainment people—a comic's manager in *Mr. Saturday Night*; a publicist on *The Larry Sanders Show* but those tend to fall into his usual type: obsequious doormats. Producers don't have to kowtow to anyone, so playing them lets Paymer unleash his inner hard-ass.

As Dan Enright in *Quiz Show* (in which, it must be noted, the Hey! It's That Guy!s are thick on the ground), he is brutal in his dismissal of used-up trivia buff Herb Stempel (John Turturro); at least there, Paymer's character is made to take a dive—much as his game-show contestants did—to protect the network from charges that it had intentionally fixed *21*. As embattled film producer Marty Rossen in *State and Main*, he blows into small-town Vermont like L.A. personified, effortlessly tossing off such charming *mots* as "I'm going to rip your heart out. Then I'm going to piss

Howard the Duck
Larry, Scientist
1986

Mr. Saturday Night
Stan
1992

Quiz Show
Dan Enright
1994

Crazy People
George
1990

The Larry Sanders Show
Norman Litkey
1992–1998

on your lungs through the hole in your chest!" Charming? No. It's the actors' job to be charming. It's the producer's job to get shit done, and Paymer's producers do not have time to take any crap.

Perhaps it was off the force of his performance as Marty that someone at ABC thought Paymer would make a convincing Irish mobster in its short-lived TV series *Line of Fire*. That someone was wrong and has probably since been fired. Paymer's Jonah Malloy acted more like a bookkeeper with acid reflux than the intimidating head of a criminal enterprise.

No, Paymer's real gift is for playing soft-spoken or ineffectual Ziggy types: George, the "Hello" guy from *Crazy People*; Leo Devoe, the ill-fated dry cleaner in *Get Shorty*; Ira Shalowitz, the excitable ice-cream magnate in the *City Slickers* movies. He accepts this; we accept it, too. Still, that doesn't mean we don't occasionally enjoy seeing him put on his steely look and make a P.A. cry.

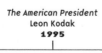

The American President
Leon Kodak
1995

Amistad
Secretary Forsyth
1997

School of Life
Matt Warner
2005

Nixon
Ron Ziegler
1995

The Hurricane
Myron Bedlock
1999

Jeffrey Tambor

HEY! IT'S THAT STUFFY, SUPERCILIOUS SIDEKICK!

ICONIC ROLE

Most actors are happy to create one iconic role in their lifetime. Jeffrey Tambor has three, and counting.

First, there's the cross-dressing Judge Alan Wachtel on **Hill Street Blues**. Then, more than a decade later, came Hank Kingsley, the Ed McMahon–spoofing, "Hey now!"–spouting windbag of a sidekick on **The Larry Sanders Show**. But then Tambor unveiled a marvelous new character: the vainglorious George Bluth Sr. on the sitcom **Arrested Development**.

And to think Tambor was once best known to many of us as the unofficial fifth Beatle of **Three's Company**, appearing in four separate episodes as three different characters. He then landed on the *Three's Company* spinoff, **The Ropers**, which promptly spun off into oblivion. He spent the next decade playing stuffy, supercilious men and, in his spare time, being confused with onetime *M*A*S*H* star David Ogden Stiers.

Tambor still nurtures his Hey! It's That Guy! gig on the side (as, for example, the Mayor of Whoville in **How the Grinch Stole Christmas**), but seriously, he could retire tomorrow and look back with nothing but pride. If he ever does decide to call it quits, we'll make sure the most palatial suite in the Hey! It's That Guy! rest home is prepped and waiting for him.

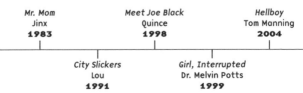

Mr. Mom	Meet Joe Black	Hellboy
Jinx	Quince	Tom Manning
1983	**1998**	**2004**

City Slickers	Girl, Interrupted
Lou	Dr. Melvin Potts
1991	**1999**

Robert Wuhl

HEY! IT'S THAT INSUFFERABLE
AGENT!

AWARD WINNER

On the one hand, you have to pity Hollywood agents. Have you ever seen a sympathetic portrait of an agent? Are there any movies or TV shows in which an agent is portrayed as anything other than moneygrubbing, insincere, and remorselessly amoral? How do you think that makes agents feel? After all, the actors and writers and directors who create those unflattering portrayals, every one of them, has an agent. Talk about ingratitude.

On the other hand, you don't have to pity Hollywood agents because, well, *they're Hollywood agents*. They are, by their nature, repellent!

Even in a show in which an agent was the lead character, ***Arli$$***, the guy was a total jerk. You wanna talk about moneygrubbing: He's got two dollar signs right in his name! Granted, he was a sports agent, not a talent agent. Like that's any better. Did you see *Jerry Maguire*?

So, who better to portray this unlikable lump than Robert Wuhl, a man who's made a career of playing weasels, sidekicks, and weasely sidekicks. You may remember him as Larry, the manager's wingman in ***Bull Durham***; as Alexander Knox, the meddlesome reporter in ***Batman***; or as an Army guy in ***Good Morning, Vietnam***. *Arli$$* went largely unloved, but Wuhl parlayed that gig into a comfy recurring spot on ***The New Hollywood Squares***. How did he do that? He must have a really good agent.

Flashdance	*Bull Durham*	*Cobb*
Mawby's Regular	Larry Hockett	Al Stump
1983	**1988**	**1994**

Good Morning, Vietnam	*The Bodyguard*
Sgt. Marty Lee Dreiwitz	Oscar Host
1987	**1992**

On the surface, everything here in the suburbs is picture-perfect, straight out of a book of Levittown model homes. But scratch the surface just a little and . . . damn. That seemingly perfect stay-at-home mom? Pill-popper. The impossibly tall, jocular young dad? Closeted. That teenager who always does so well in school? Killed two people in a hospital emergency room. And that elegant older lady spent a *lot* of time in a loony bin. As for the swarthy fellow with the huge eye-

THE SUBURBS

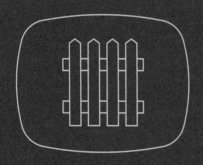

brows, let's just say he's got a suspicious number of friends in waste manage-ment—*and* he never mows his lawn. What do you mean, "Is that it"? Isn't that enough? And anyway, no, that's not all. But in order to get more details than that, you'll have to check in with the neighborhood gossip, who sees all and knows all.

Caroline Aaron

POSSE MEMBER

AS SEEN ON TV

HEY! IT'S THAT NEIGHBORLY **BEST FRIEND!**

There's an episode of *Law & Order* involving a woman who kills a liquor salesman, supposedly because he attempted to rape her. The suspect is apprehended based on a tip from a woman who saw her in a pub washroom before the murder; the tipster tells police they had discussed the Jacques Dessange cosmetics the suspect had on and adds, "Her makeup was flawless."

That tipster was played by Caroline Aaron.

Aaron kicked off her career with *Come Back to the Five and Dime, Jimmy Dean, Jimmy Dean*, and has since appeared in such films as *Working Girl*, *Edward Scissorhands*, and *Sleepless in Seattle*. Her slightly gravelly voice, deadpan delivery, and everywoman looks also seem to have endeared her to Woody Allen—she is a veteran of his films. Her showiest role in a Woody Allen film came with *Crimes and Misdemeanors*, in which she played Allen's character's sister—the one whose blind date tied her down to a bed and, not to put too fine a point on it, pooped on her.

Aaron has been canny enough to supplement her roles in Woody Allen movies by playing no-bullshit Jewish women in such films as *This Is My Life* and *Primary Colors*. As long as leading ladies need sassy, non-WASP best friends—and Lainie Kazan is too old—Caroline Aaron will have work.

Sleepless in Seattle
Dr. Marcia Fieldstone
1993

Primary Colors
Thomas Putnam
1998

Bounce
Donna
2000

Big Night
Woman in Restaurant
1996

Anywhere But Here
Gail Letterfine
1999

Kathy Baker

**HEY! IT'S THAT
CORDIAL BUT CONNIVING
NEIGHBOR LADY!**

AWARD WINNER

PERIOD PIECE

VILLAIN

We just don't trust Kathy Baker. Maybe she's a nice lady. Maybe she really means it when she says "Welcome to the neighborhood" and holds out that big basket of scones. But you know she's hiding something—like maybe a *fake hand*!?!

She did just that on ***Boston Public***, the TV series from producer David E. Kelley, in which Baker played a cold shrew who tortured her son, then cut off her own hand with a chainsaw.

In fact, Kathy Baker's got the sleazy, horny neighbor-lady thing down cold, with or without prosthetics. You might remember her from ***Edward Scissorhands***, in which she played "Joyce Monroe, Neighbor."

We're not really sure why Kathy Baker makes such a good conniving meddler. She's certainly proved she can play very nice neighbors—even upstanding citizens. She was a perfectly kind mom in ***13 Going on 30*** and a perfectly lovely neighbor lady in ***Cold Mountain***.

But for whatever reason, if there's a movie or TV show or TV movie set in a small town that's not quite what it seems, or a sleepy community that's suddenly gripped by conflict because certain people just can't keep their noses out of other people's business . . . well, don't be surprised if one of those business-smeared noses belongs to Kathy Baker.

The Right Stuff
Louise Shepard
1983

Mad Dog and Glory
Lee
1993

Cold Mountain
Sally Swanger
2003

Picket Fences
Dr. Jill Brock
1992–1996

The Cider House Rules
Nurse Angela
1999

Craig Bierko

Stats:

HEY! IT'S THAT SMARMY YET
ODDLY CORNY DAD!

PERIOD PIECE

NEW SCHOOL

Like Christopher McDonald (page 190), Craig Bierko's niche involves both corniness and smarm: a sort of earnest insincerity. The role that best exemplifies this attitude is the titular one in *The Music Man* (on Broadway), in which con man "Professor" Harold Hill must win over the town of River City by acting like a fast-talking, old-fashioned reactionary (raging against such illicit youth activities as—gasp!—pool!). Bierko sells his smarm with a big, toothy smile and a knowing wink.

Bierko was corny in the way that only sitcoms demand as a cast member on the short-lived series *Sydney*, *Madman of the People*, and *Pride and Joy*; he switched it up to play a smarmy Hollywood talent agent on *Mad About You* and a smarmy porkpie-hat-wearing dork of a Carrie Bradshaw love interest on *Sex and the City*. He was smarmy as a reporter on the short-lived *The Court*; corny as a horror-movie protagonist in *The Thirteenth Floor*; and spectacularly corny as a young dad in *Dickie Roberts: Former Child Star*.

Will any future Bierko role marry smarm and corniness as seamlessly as *The Music Man*? Probably not. Unless someone writes a movie in which McDonald and Bierko play con-artist brothers. Wouldn't *Matchstick Men* have been that much more appealing if it had them in the title roles and absolutely no Nicolas Cage? That's a rhetorical question, obviously.

'Til There Was You
Jon Haas
1997

Fear and Loathing in Las Vegas
Lacerda
1998

Cinderella Man
Max Baer
2005

Sour Grapes
Richie Maxwell
1998

The Thirteenth Floor
Douglas Hall/John Ferguson/David
1999

Paul Dooley

HEY! IT'S THAT SHAMBLING, ## WELL-MEANING DAD!

Stats: **BALD**

AS SEEN ON TV

DOUBLE THREAT

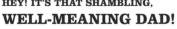

Adults in John Hughes teen movies don't usually come off too well. Occasionally, though, Hughes writes an adult character who treats the teen protagonist with love and respect.

There is a moment, in *Sixteen Candles*, when a father, in the midst of planning a hellish wedding for his elder daughter, hangs out with his forgotten middle child (played by Molly Ringwald) and ruefully talks shit about his future in-laws. It's a genuine moment (another rare thing in a John Hughes movie), and the actor who makes it work—wearing a bathrobe and a hangdog expression—is Paul Dooley.

Playing secondary dad characters to heroic daughters is what he does most and best. He's been a dad to Julia Roberts (*Runaway Bride*), Toni Collette (*Clockwatchers*), Sherry Stringfield (*ER*), Bess Armstrong (*My So-Called Life*), and Cheryl Hines (*Curb Your Enthusiasm*), and he originated the role of Gus Stemple (father to Helen Hunt's Jamie) on *Mad About You*.

When not playing some pulchritudinous actress's dad, Paul Dooley plays judges. He has done so in *Happy, Texas*, on *Dharma & Greg*, and, most recently, on *The Practice*.

The natural next step for Paul Dooley is to play Amy Brenneman's dad on *Judging Amy*.

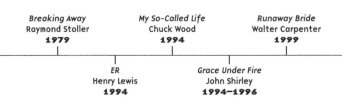

Breaking Away		*My So-Called Life*		*Runaway Bride*
Raymond Stoller		Chuck Wood		Walter Carpenter
1979		**1994**		**1999**
	ER		*Grace Under Fire*	
	Henry Lewis		John Shirley	
	1994		**1994–1996**	

Brian Doyle-Murray

Stats: AWARD WINNER

HEY! IT'S THAT
BLUSTERY MAYOR!

You could say, "Oh, Brian Doyle-Murray, he's Bill Murray's brother." You could say, "He just gets parts in all of Bill's films, like *Caddyshack*, *Scrooged*, and *Groundhog Day*." You could say that, but why would you want to?

Brian Doyle-Murray is, of course, Bill Murray's brother, but other than the surname, there's not much resemblance. Whereas Bill became a star playing laconic wiseasses, Brian is more inclined toward officious bureaucrats. He's played mayors, coaches, colonels, and ministers—basically, blustery authority figures and assorted blowhards.

You might say that Brian Doyle-Murray is a comedian's comedian, because wherever you find good humor, he'll be there. Go ahead: Name a funny film from the past twenty years. *Waiting for Guffman*? He's in it. *Wayne's World*? He's there, too. *National Lampoon's Vacation*? Wouldn't be the same without him. *Sixteen Candles*? Thoroughly Doyle-ified. He's livened up some TV comedies, too: the cult Chris Elliott TV series *Get a Life*? Very high in vitamin B.D.M.

And, of course, he's often found in close proximity to Bill Murray. But that's probably because, you know, they're brothers.

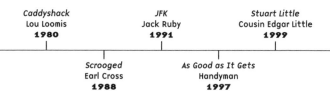

Caddyshack
Lou Loomis
1980

JFK
Jack Ruby
1991

Stuart Little
Cousin Edgar Little
1999

Scrooged
Earl Cross
1988

As Good as It Gets
Handyman
1997

Bruce Greenwood

Stats: CANADIAN

NEW SCHOOL

HEY! IT'S THAT UNTRUSTWORTHY, TWO-TIMING, BOO-HISS HUSBAND!

You wouldn't think Bruce Greenwood is a bad guy just to look at him. He doesn't sport a pencil-thin mustache. He doesn't wear a stovepipe hat. He's not often spotted, to our knowledge, rubbing his hands with evil glee.

Plus, if you've seen him in any of Atom Egoyan's fine films, you know he's an actor of remarkable range. Take his Fu Manchu–wearing trucker in *The Sweet Hereafter*, or his tragic dad in *Exotica*. No one-dimensional cackler, this guy.

So why, oh why, is he continually cast as evil jackasses in Hollywood?

For if you know Bruce Greenwood, chances are you know him as a jerk or a cad or a boor or a cheat. He played Ashley Judd's evil, wife-framing scoundrel of a husband in *Double Jeopardy*. He played an evil, cuckolded Internal Affairs weasel in *Hollywood Homicide*. He played a slippery, duplicitous corporate crook in *I, Robot*.

And he does this all very well, no doubt. Greenwood's a versatile, talented actor who, for some reason, gets consistently cast as vacant, soulless fiends. Maybe it's because he's Canadian. In any case, we'd love to see him in a Fu Manchu mustache again, or any other mustache, for that matter, as long as it's not the pencil-thin Snidely Whiplash type.

Nowhere Man
Thomas Veil
1995

Thirteen Days
President John F. Kennedy
2000

Being Julia
Lord Charles
2004

Double Jeopardy
Nick Parsons
1999

The Core
Col. Robert Iverson
2003

HEY! IT'S CHAPTER THIRTEEN: THE SUBURBS

Dan Hedaya

HEY! IT'S THAT SMARMY, SLIGHTLY
GREASY BAD NEIGHBOR
(WITH FIVE O'CLOCK SHADOW)!

Dan Hedaya plays weaselly, unkempt, shady characters. Even if you don't like to judge a man by his appearance, there's something about Hedaya's manner and grooming that make you think he's not entirely on the level. He lurches. He mumbles. He slurs. He rants. (He was, therefore, an excellent choice to play President Richard Nixon in the underrated *Dick*; who's shadier or more five o'clock shadowy than Tricky Dick?)

Hedaya has found himself, as he approaches his twilight years, in cinema's suburbs—as in, for instance, *To Die For*. Hedaya plays Joe Maretto, father-in-law to Nicole Kidman's dim yet ambitious Suzanne Stone-Maretto. The thoroughly WASPy Suzanne gets off several casually offensive lines at the expense of her in-laws' Italian ancestry, and it is suggested by some of her relatives that the Marettos may be . . . well, "connected"—a charge they vehemently deny. But in the end, the charge proves true, as it is strongly implied that Joe has arranged for Suzanne to be professionally dispatched (by David Cronenberg!). Hedaya may seem to

Blood Simple
Julian Marty
1984

The Addams Family
Tully Alford,
Addams Family's Attorney
1991

The First Wives Club
Morton Cushman
1996

Joe Versus the Volcano
Mr. Frank Waturi
1990

To Die For
Joe Maretto
1995

be playing an upstanding family man, but it's just never a good idea to assume he's totally legit.

Hedaya has, in recent years, made moves to expand his dramatic range by taking on roles like Alicia Silverstone's father in *Clueless*. Leaving aside the fact that it was the least believable parent-child casting since Sally Field and Tom Hanks in *Forrest Gump*, Hedaya's Mel Horowitz actually is a departure from his usual hood-ish lout; unlike Nick Tortelli on *Cheers* (and its short-lived spin-off *The Tortellis*), Mel isn't dumb or venal. Well, maybe a tiny bit venal. He is a Los Angeles lawyer, after all.

But Mel is an anomaly. In general, Hedaya is most often called upon to play neighborhood creeps: dirty cops (*The Hurricane*), unpleasant coaches (*Swimfan*), soul-killing bosses (*Joe Versus the Volcano*). He may not have played suburban reformed crack whore Jerri Blank's father in the TV version of *Strangers with Candy*, but installing him in the role for the feature film was exactly right.

Dick
President Richard M.
"Dick" Nixon
1999

Yes, Dear
Don Ludke
2000–2003

Strangers with Candy
Guy Blank
2005

The Hurricane
Det. Sgt. Della Pesca
1999

Swimfan
Coach Simkins
2002

Dana Ivey

Stats: AS SEEN ON TV

HEY! IT'S THAT CONSTIPATED, DISAPPROVING MATRON!

Dana Ivey appears in **Legally Blonde 2** as Congresswoman Libby Hauser, a forbidding authority figure won over by Reese Witherspoon's Elle Woods when she points out that both she and Libby are alumnae of the same sorority. Why impress a legislator with sound legal arguments when you could accomplish the same thing by doing an inane dance routine with her instead?

Sometimes, Ivey gets cast in a film to transition from disapproval to loving acceptance: In **The Addams Family**, she starts out a tight-assed WASPy type who meets Cousin It and drops her patrician disapproval as she melts into love. Other times, her disapproval remains fixed—as in **Two Weeks Notice**, where playing Sandra Bullock's mother requires her to glower angrily at Bullock's boss, played by Hugh Grant. Still other times, Ivey is disapproving as a character in a service position—like an executive assistant in the 1995 remake of **Sabrina**—so that she can act as a kind of Greek chorus, a surrogate for the audience's disapproval.

Most films would benefit from a little bit of Dana Ivey expressing her disgust at the proceedings.

Dirty Rotten Scoundrels
Mrs. Reed
1988

The Scarlet Letter
Meredith Stonehall
1995

Orange County
Vera Gantner
2002

Sleepless in Seattle
Mrs. Reed
1993

The Impostors
Mrs. Essendine
1998

David Krumholtz

MULTI-ETHNIC

AS SEEN ON TV

PERIOD PIECE

NEW SCHOOL

HEY! IT'S THAT
NICE JEWISH BOY!

The kid has a quality. You see him and you are instantly reminded of five things you've seen him in. At least, that was true a couple of years ago, when he appeared in one of the highest-profile roles of his career—Paul Sobriki, the schizophrenic patient who stabbed two doctors on *ER*. All the talk around the water cooler the next day was, "Where have I seen that kid before? Wasn't he Tobey Maguire's jerk-ass druggie roommate in *The Ice Storm*?" "Oh yeah! And he was Christina Ricci's boyfriend in *Addams Family Values*!" "Wait, wasn't he the head elf in *The Santa Clause*? What's that guy's name?"

Partly it's his face—his thick eyebrows and big old schnozz made him look like a middle-aged character actor even when he played a spoiled child star in *Life with Mikey* at the tender age of . . . okay, 15. But still. And because you can remember so many of the movies in which he's appeared—*Slums of Beverly Hills*, *Sidewalks of New York*, *The Mexican*, plus *The Trouble with Normal*, *Chicago Sons*, and *The Lyon's Den*, three of his many unsuccessful TV series, you think he must have been working like a fiend for years. But he hasn't.

He has a quality—or maybe he has a schnozz—that makes you remember when you've seen him, even if you never plan to remember his name. And that is what they call a Hey! It's That Guy!

Life with Mikey Barry Corman **1993**	*Bulworth* Dennis Murphy **1998**	*Numb3rs* Charlie Eppes **2005**
Slums of Beverly Hills Ben Abromowitz **1998**	*Liberty Heights* Yussel **1999**	

Nancy Lenehan

HEY! IT'S THAT PERKY, PERFECT **PARENT!**

Those of us who grew up with mothers who worked outside the home (and we say this without any bitterness or resentment; we love our moms and couldn't be prouder of their professional achievements) sometimes regard portrayals of at-home moms in pop culture with a wistful sigh. Watching virtually any Nancy Lenehan performance makes us yearn for what might have been.

Lenehan plays perfect moms. In fact, Lenehan has perfected the role of the too-perfect mom: the mom who does everything right so effortlessly with her kids that the other moms feel inferior. Her blunt-cut blonde bob demonstrates that, while she recognizes the need to look presentable, she doesn't spend time fussing with her own looks. Why should she, when she could, instead, be ironing Sissie's cheerleading uniform? Her sunny, unflappable, WASPy demeanor assures the world that, while her sphere of influence may be constrained compared with those of her college friends, who went on to become lawyers or marketing executives, she is solidly happy and content; no secret depression or drinking problem for her! (This

She's Having a Baby
Cynthia
1988

The Great Outdoors
Waitress
1988

Grace Under Fire
Mrs. Sheffield
1993–1998

Buffy the Vampire Slayer
Cynthia in "Dead Man's Party"
1998

Pleasantville
Marge Jenkins
1998

is why you see her on cheery, superficial sitcoms like **Malcolm in the Middle** and **Everybody Loves Raymond**, as opposed to dark dramas or alarmist TV movies.) On the rare occasions when Lenehan doesn't play "X's Mom" or "Mrs. Y," she still can't stray far from the kids, in roles like "Principal" on **Ally McBeal**, "Teacher" in **Eddie's Million Dollar Cook-Off**, or "School Secretary" on **Jack & Bobby**.

But those are deviations from the norm: Lenehan's been playing soccer moms since before the term even existed. And it seems as though Lenehan's particular niche as an actor was clear right from the start; though there's a somewhat glamorous-sounding "Young Woman" (in **Emergency Room** in 1983), she'd already been a "Mother in Supermarket" by then (**Jekyll & Hyde . . . Together Again** in 1982), and soon went on to such Lenehan-sounding roles as Mrs. Barton, Connie, Blanche, Marge Jenkins, and the like—sturdy, sweet-natured mothers straight outta Darien, Connecticut, and Winnetka, Illinois.

Felicity
Faye Rotundi
1998–2001

Catch Me If You Can
Carol Strong
2002

Human Nature
Puff's Mother
2001

Married to the Kellys
Sandy Kelly
2003–2004

Sam McMurray

HEY! IT'S THAT BACKSLAPPING
JACKASS!

Sam McMurray has slapped many a back in his time. In fact, he created what now stands as the Platonic ideal of backslapping jackasses, with his role as the leering, wife-swapping, monster-brat-raising Glen in the Coen brothers' *Raising Arizona*. (This was the man who commends his son's facility with the alphabet after spotting him carving the word FART into the wall of Nicolas Cage's trailer.)

The grating chortle; the leering sneer; the expert grasp of puffed-up, overly loud, and ultimately empty bonhomie—these are the bricks with which McMurray built the foundation of his career. McMurray has animated such repellent characters as Don Buckman in *Addams Family Values*, Lester Leeman in *Drop Dead Gorgeous*, and Doug, Chandler's unfunny, loathsome boss on *Friends*. (Not to offend the Dons, Dougs, and Glens out there, but it's impossible to overlook the fact that these are the official names for jerks in Hollywood.) He even played a character named Skip Wankman, in 1992's *Class Act*—which, we're guessing, Wankman was not.

So to the Dons, Dougs, and Glens of the world, we can only say this: At least your surname's not Wankman. Unless, of course, it is Wankman, in which case, you get our deepest sympathies.

Raising Arizona Glen **1987**	*Baby Geniuses* Goon Bob **1999**	*The King of Queens* Supervisor O'Boyle **2001**
National Lampoon's Christmas Vacation Bill **1989**	*The Mod Squad* Detective Tricky **1999**	

Robin Thomas

Stats: VILLAIN

HEY! IT'S THAT
SIMPERING PISSANT!

AS SEEN ON TV

STRAIGHT-TO-VIDEO

An open letter from J. T. Walsh:

So that's what you've come to? You have to give space to skinny little whipped pissants like Robin Thomas?

That's none of my business? I'm J. T. fucking Walsh, *friend*, and if anyone knows what makes a Hey! It's That Guy!, I do.

It all started with *Murphy Brown*. First of all, Murphy was one of those women's libbers, like Maude, except you wanted to screw her. So you get this character, single broad. Producers get her in trouble. Gotta give her a boyfriend. So they give her two, and one of them's your bitch-boy, Robin Thomas, a bleeding-heart sensitive liberal type. Sure enough, he's the father. But he can't be a stand-up guy—takes off, and we never see him again, because he's off in Bolivia or Costa Rica or some damn place, licking his wounds because the producers found a way to figuratively castrate him.

So now, he's a eunuch. He's got to live it down. Can't. Gets cast in *The Contender*; the title character is this powerful woman (another libber, *of course*), and then she's got this nothing husband played by . . . yep. Which brings us to *The Banger Sisters*. This time, at least, he plays a husband who's been oppressing Susan Sarandon. So his character is still a bland suburban wuss, but maybe he's a little bit of a son-of-a-bitch, too. I'll take that.

Another World Mark Singleton **1983–1985**	*The Mommies* Paul Kellogg **1993–1994**	*The Banger Sisters* Raymond Kingsley **2002**

Summer School Vice-Principal Phil Gills **1987**	*Star Maps* Martin **1997**

Celia Weston

HEY! IT'S THAT VINTAGE SOUTHERN BELLE/LOCKJAWED
NEW ENGLAND MATRIARCH!

Celia Weston is tall, blonde, and Southern. While not a classic beauty à la Catherine Deneuve, she possesses the handsome, stately elegance that calls to mind a Southern belle. As such, Weston tends to play two particular types of characters, for whom appearing to be "done up" at all times is *de rigueur*.

First: blowsy Southern dames. She starred on *Alice* (filling the "sassy Southern waitress" quota after the departure of Polly "Kiss My Grits" Holliday) and in *Dead Man Walking* (as the mother of one of Sean Penn's murder victims), *Flirting with Disaster* (as Ben Stiller's biological mother— or is she?), and *K-PAX* (as an aging mental patient). The last of these, in fact, is practically a parody of all blowsy Southern dames; Weston plays a Miss Havisham–esque hospital inmate who, in her dementia, still makes up her face and puts on her costume jewelry and sets her table as if eternally expecting a gentleman caller. She's so blowsy, she's blown her sanity clear on out the door, Big Daddy.

| | *Alice* Jolene Hunnicutt **1981–1985** | | *Dead Man Walking* Mary Beth Percy **1995** | | *The Talented Mr. Ripley* Aunt Joan **1999** |

| *Little Man Tate* Miss Nimvel **1991** | | *Flirting with Disaster* Valerie Swaney **1996** |

Then: snooty upper-class ladies, as in *The Talented Mr. Ripley* (in which Weston plays Cate Blanchett's rich aunt), *Joe Gould's Secret* (as a coolly professional receptionist at the '50s-era *New Yorker*), and *In the Bedroom* (as an insensitive family friend to Sissy Spacek and Tom Wilkinson). It's fun to watch her swanning about in *Flirting with Disaster*, dripping with gold jewelry, calling her grandson a "cracker," and never too far from her tumbler of bourbon, all, "Not the Chinese zodiac!" It's just as much fun to see her purse up those stately lips and broadcast her bitter New England disapproval at the homeless Ian Holm in *Joe Gould's Secret*.

We never would have thought that the blowsy dame and the frigid matron were two sides of the same dramatic coin. Celia Weston has ensured that we'll never make that mistake again.

Joe Gould's Secret
Sarah
2000

K-PAX
Doris Archer
2001

The Village
Vivian Percy
2004

In the Bedroom
Katie Grinnel
2001

Far from Heaven
Mona Lauder
2002

GENERAL INDEX

Page numbers in **bold** (for example, 250) indicate color photographs.

214

TV SHOW & MOVIE TITLE INDEX

PHOTO CREDITS

p. 16: *Full Metal Jacket*, Adam Baldwin, 1987.

p. 17: *Article 99*, Keith David, 1992, © Orion Pictures Corporation/courtesy Everett Collection.

p. 18: *Land of Plenty*, (aka *Terre Dabondance*), John Diehl, 2004, © IFC Films/courtesy Everett Collection.

p. 19: *Full Metal Jacket*, Lee Ermey, 1987.

p. 20: *Seaquest DSV*, Michael Ironside, 1993–95. © Universal TV/courtesy Everett Collection.

p. 21: *Reagans*, Zeljko Ivanek, 2003. © SHOWTIME/courtesy Everett Collection.

p. 22: *Raise Your Voice*, David Keith, 2004, © New Line/courtesy Everett Collection.

p. 23: *Scrubs*, John C. McGinley, season 1, 2001–.

p. 24: *The Walking Dead*, Joe Morton, 1995. © Savoy Pictures/courtesy Everett Collection.

p. 25: Leland Orser at premiere of Peter Berg's *Very Bad Things*, New York, November 11, 1998. Photo: Sean Roberts/Everett Collection.

p. 26: *Robocop 3*, Daniel Von Bargen, 1993. © Orion Pictures Corporation/courtesy Everett Collection.

p. 30: *Mitchell*, Joe Don Baker, 1975.

p. 32: Patrick Cranshaw at the 76th annual *Academy Awards*, February 29, 2004, photo by Craig Sjodin. ABC/courtesy Everett Collection.

p. 33: *The Lord of the Rings: Two Towers*, Brad Dourif, 2002, © New Line/courtesy Everett Collection.

p. 34: *V.I. Warshawski*, Charles Durning, 1991. © Buena Vista Pictures/courtesy Everett Collection.

p. 36: *UC: Undercover*, William Forsythe, 2001–present.

p. 38: *No Code of Conduct*, Courtney Gains, 1998. © Dimension Films/courtesy Everett Collection.

p. 39: *EdTV*, Clint Howard, 1999.

p. 40: *Natural Born Killers*, O-Lan Jones, DVD still courtesy of Edward Dormer, Philadelphia.

p. 41: *Bubble Boy*, John Carroll Lynch, 2001.

p. 42: *O Brother, Where Art Thou?*, Tim Blake Nelson, 2000.

p. 43: *Bonnie and Clyde*, Michael J. Pollard, 1967.

p. 44: *Henry: Portrait of a Serial Killer*, Michael Rooker, 1986.

p. 45: *Repo Man*, Tracy Walter, 1984.

p. 48: *Anniversary Party*, Jane Adams, 2001.

p. 49: *Welcome to New York*, 2000–2001.

Christine Baranski.

p. 50: *A Cinderella Story*, Jennifer Coolidge, 2004, © Warner Brothers/courtesy Everett Collection.

p. 52: *House of Sand and Fog*, Frances Fisher, 2003, © DreamWorks/courtesy Everett Collection.

p. 53: Lee Garlington © Mario Casilli/Shooting Star.

p. 54: *The Hebrew Hammer*, Adam Goldberg, 2003, © Strand Releasing/courtesy Everett Collection.

p. 56: *Hexed*, Ayre Gross, 1993, © Columbia/courtesy Everett Collection.

p. 57: *25th Hour*, Philip Seymour Hoffman, 2002, © Walt Disney/courtesy Everett Collection.

p. 58: *Criminal*, John C. Reilly, 2004, © Warner Independent/courtesy Everett Collection.

p. 60: *Dead Birds*, Isaiah Washington, 2004.

p. 61: *Big Trouble in Little China*, Victory Wong, DVD still courtesy of Edward Dormer, Philadelphia.

p. 64: *Unstrung Heroes*, Maury Chaykin, 1995. © Buena Vista Pictures/courtesy Everett Collection.

p. 65: Tovah Feldshuh arrives to the private screening of *Fahrenheit 9/11* at the Ziegfeld Theater in New York, June 14, 2004. Photo by Brad Barket/The Everett Collection.

p. 66: *The Client*, John Heard, 1995–96. © Warner Bros. Television/courtesy Everett Collection.

p. 68: *Six Feet Under*, Richard Jenkins, season 3, 2001–. © HBO/courtesy Everett Collection.

p. 70: *Auto Focus*, Ron Leibman, 2002, © Sony Pictures Classics/courtesy Everett Collection.

p. 71: *Runaway Jury*, Bruce McGill, 2003. ™ & © 20th Century Fox Film Corp. All rights reserved.

p. 72: *Oz*, Austin Pendleton, 1997–present. © HBO/courtesy Everett Collection.

p. 73: *Queens Supreme*, Oliver Platt, season 1, 2003.

p. 74: *Alias*, Ron Rifkin, Reunion (season 3, aired October 12, 2003), 2001–. Photo: ABC/Carin Baer, © ABC/courtesy Everett Collection.

p. 75: *The Practice*, Holland Taylor, Free Dental (season 4), 1994–2004. © ABC/courtesy Everett Collection.

p. 78: *The Sopranos*, James Gandolfini, television. Season 2. 1999–.

p. 80: *The Sopranos*, Michael Imperioli, (sea-

son 5, episode 53, Two Tonys, March 7, 2004), 1999–. © HBO/courtesy Everett Collection.

p. 81: *That's Life*, Debi Mazar, 2000–2002.

p. 82: *The Godfather*, Alex Rocco, 1972.

p. 83: *The Wedding Singer*, Frank Sivero, DVD still courtesy of Edward Dormer, Philadelphia.

p. 84: *Ed*, Mike Starr, 2000–2004.

p. 85: *The Sopranos*, season 5, Aida Turturro, 1999–. © HBO/courtesy Everett Collection.

p. 86: *This Thing of Ours*, Frank Vincent, 2003, © Small Planet/courtesy Everett Collection.

p. 87: *Analyze That*, Joe Viterelli, 2002, © Warner Brothers/courtesy Everett Collection.

p. 90: *24* (aka *Twenty-Four*), 2001–present, Xander Berkeley.

p. 91: *Citizen Baines*, James Cromwell, 2001.

p. 92: *Runaway Jury*, Bruce Davison, 2003, ™ & © 20th Century Fox Film Corp. All rights reserved.

p. 93: *Alias*, (Cipher, Season 2), Victor Garber, 2001–present.

p. 94: *Dogville*, Philip Baker Hall, 2003, © Lions Gate/courtesy Everett Collection.

p. 95: *Two Over Easy*, Lucinda Jenney, 1994. © Showtime Networks/courtesy Everett Collection.

p. 96: *Cross of Fire*, Donald Moffat, 1989. © NBC/courtesy Everett Collection.

p. 97: *The Agency*, 2001–03, Will Patton, © CBS/courtesy Everett Collection.

p. 98: *Head of State*, James Rebhorn, 2003, © DreamWorks/courtesy Everett Collection.

p. 99: *Beach Bums*, director Saul Rubinek, 2001, candid on set.

p. 100: *Die Hard 2*, Senator Fred Thompson, 1990, ™ & © 20th Century Fox Film Corp. All rights reserved. Courtesy Everett Collection.

p. 102: Breakdown, J. T. Walsh, 1997.

p. 103: *24* (aka *Twenty-Four*), episode 8:00–9:00, season 2), Harris Yulin. © 2003 Fox Broadcasting Co.

p. 106: *Planet of the Apes*, Erick Avari, 2001. ™ & © 20th Century Fox Film Corp. All rights reserved.

p. 107: *Goldeneye*, Sean Bean, 1995, © United Artists/courtesy Everett Collection.

p. 108: *Reservoir Dogs*, Steve Buscemi, 1992.

p. 110: *Rules of Attraction*, Clifton Collins Jr., 2002, © Lions Gate/courtesy Everett Collection.

p. 111: *License to Kill*, Robert Davi, 1989.

p. 112: *The Untouchables*, Billy Drago, 1987. © Paramount Pictures/courtesy Everett Collection.

p. 114: *Meds*, William Fichtner, 2002–2003.

p. 115: Brendan Gleeson at world premiere of *A.I.: Artificial Intelligence*, New York, June 26, 2001, by CJ Contino.

p. 116: *Martin*, Jon Gries, 1992–1997. © Warner Bros./courtesy Everett Collection.

p. 117: *Traffic*, Luis Guzman, 2000, USA Films/courtesy Everett Collection.

p. 118: James Hong © Yoram Kahana/Shooting Star.

p. 119: Story of Magic, Host Ricky Jay, 1997.

p. 120: *Die Hard*, Al Leong, DVD still courtesy of Edward Dormer, Philadelphia.

p. 121: *Ransom*, Delroy Lindo, 1996.

p. 122: *Bad Company*, Peter Stormare, 2002 © Walt Disney/courtesy Everett Collection.

p. 123: *Mortal Kombat: Annihilation*, Brian Thompson, 1997. © New Line Cinema/courtesy Everett Collection.

p. 124: *Monk*, Danny Trejo. Mr. Monk Goes to Jail (season 2), 2002–. © USA Network/courtesy Everett Collection.

p. 128: *Wedding Singer*, Ellen Albertini Dow, 1998.

p. 129: To Gillian on Her 37th Birthday, Bruce Altman, 1996. © Sony Pictures/courtesy Everett Collection.

p. 130: *Picket Fences*, Amy Aquino, 1992–96. ™ & © 20th Century Fox Film Corp. All rights reserved.

p. 131: *City of Angels*, Viola Davis as Nurse Lynette Peeler, 2000.

p. 132: *Tully (Truth About Tully)*, Glenn Fitzgerald, 2000.

p. 133: Margo Martindale at screening of *Iron Jawed Angels*, New York, February 9, 2004, by Janet Mayer.

p. 134: *Spider-Man*, J. K. Simmons, 2002, © Columbia Pictures/courtesy Everett Collection.

p. 135: *Glass House*, Stellan Skarsgard, 2001.

p. 136: *Boston Public*, Joey Slotnick as Milton Buttle, 2000–04. ™ & © 20th Century Fox Film Corp. All rights reserved. Courtesy Everett Collection.

p. 140: *The Big Time*, 2002, Dylan Baker.

p. 142: *The West Wing*, Gary Cole, 1999–, season 5. © NBC/courtesy Everett Collection.

p. 144: *Big Fat Liar*, Paul Giamatti, 2002, © Universal/courtesy Everett Collection.

p. 146: *13 Going on 30*, Judy Greer, 2004, © Columbia/courtesy Everett Collection.

p. 147: *Tattingers*, Zach Grenier, 1989. © NBC/courtesy Everett Collection.

p. 148: John Michael Higgins © Tear-N Tan/Shooting Star.

p. 150: *Office Space*, Stephen Root, 1999. ™ & © 20th Century Fox Film Corp. All rights reserved. Courtesy Everett Collection.

p. 151: *JFK*, Jay O. Sanders, 1991. © Warner Bros./courtesy Everett Collection.

p. 152: *Rodney*, Nick Searcy, 2004–, photo: Bob D'Amico. © ABC/courtesy Everett Collection.

p. 153: *Groundhog Day*, Stephen Tobolowsky, 1993. © Columbia Pictures/courtesy Everett Collection.

p. 156: *Boomtown*, Gary Basaraba, 2002–2004.

p. 157: *The Shawshank Redemption*, Clancy Brown, 1994. © Columbia Pictures/courtesy Everett Collection.

p. 158: *City by the Sea*, George Dzundza, 2002. © Warner Brothers/courtesy Everett Collection.

p. 160: *Crossing Jordan*, Miguel Ferrer, Someone to Count On (season 1, aired April 29, 2002), 2001–.

p. 161: *C.S.I.*, 2000–present, Paul Guilfoyle. © CBS/courtesy Everett Collection.

p. 162: *Monk*, Ted Levine, 2002–. © USA Network/courtesy Everett Collection.

p. 163: *The Job*, Bill Nunn, 2001–02.

p. 164: *Singing Detective*, Jon Polito, 2003, © Paramount/courtesy Everett Collection.

p. 166: *The Shield*, C. C. H. Pounder, 2002–. ™ & © 20th Century Fox Film Corp. All rights reserved. Courtesy Everett Collection.

p. 170: *Article 99*, Troy Evans, 1992. © Orion Pictures/courtesy: Everett Collection.

p. 171: *The Breakfast Club*, Paul Gleason, 1985. © MCA/Universal Pictures/courtesy Everett Collection.

p. 172: *Stuart Little*, Jeffrey Jones, 1999. © Columbia Pictures/courtesy Everett Collection.

p. 174: *Forever Knight*, John Kapelos, season 2, 1994–96. © Columbia TriStar Domestic Television/courtesy Everett Collection.

p. 175: Taryn Manning at the premiere of *Sky Captain and the World of Tomorrow*, Sept. 14, 2004, in Los Angeles, California. Photo by John Hayes/Everett Collection.

p. 176: *The Hogan Family*, Edie McClurg, 1988–91.

p. 177: *Freddy vs. Jason*, Lochlyn Munro, 2003, © New Line/courtesy Everett Collection.

p. 178: *Waiting for the Light*, Vincent Schiavelli, John Bedford Lloyd, 1990.

p. 179: *Clueless*, Wallace Shawn, 1996–99. © Paramount/courtesy Everett Collection.

p. 180: *Down Home*, Gedde Watanabe, 1990–91. © NBC/courtesy Everett Collection.

p. 181: *Matt Houston*, George Wyner, 1982–85. © Warner Bros./courtesy Everett Collection.

p. 184: *The Day of the Locust*, William Atherton, 1975.

p. 185: *Waiting for Guffman*, Bob Balaban, 1997.

p. 186: *In the Soup*, Seymour Cassel, 1992. © Triton Pictures/courtesy Everett Collection.

p. 188: Judah Friedlander at IFP Gotham Awards, September 23, 2003, New York, by Janet Mayer.

p. 189: *The Beast*, Harriet Sansom Harris, 2001.

p. 190: *Cracking Up*, Chris McDonald, season 1, 2004–. ™ & copyright © 20th Century Fox Film Corp. All rights reserved. Courtesy Everett Collection.

p. 191: *A Mighty Wind*, Larry Miller, 2003, © Warner Brothers/courtesy Everett Collection.

p. 192: *Quiz Show*, David Paymer, 1994. © Hollywood Pictures/courtesy Everett Collection.

p. 194: *Hellboy*, Jeffrey Tambor, 2004, © Columbia/courtesy Everett Collection.

p. 195: *Arliss* aka *Arli$$* Robert Wuhl, 1996–2002. © HBO/courtesy Everett Collection.

p. 198: Caroline Aaron during the AFI Fest 2004 opening night premiere of *Beyond the Sea*, November 4, 2004. Photo by Michael Germana/Everett Collection.

p. 199: *Sanctuary*, Kathy Baker, aired February 28, 2001. 2001.

p. 200: *Sour Grapes*, Craig Bierko, 1998. © Castle Rock Entertainment/courtesy Everett Collection.

p. 201: *Breaking Away*, Paul Dooley, 1979, ™ and © 20th Century Fox Film Corp. All rights reserved.

p. 202: *Groundhog Day*, Brian Doyle-Murray, 1993. © Columbia/courtesy Everett Collection.

p. 203: *Hollywood Homicide*, Bruce Greenwood, 2003, © Columbia/courtesy Everett Collection.

p. 204: *A Night at the Roxbury*, Dan Hedaya, 1998. © Paramount Pictures/courtesy Everett Collection.

p. 206: *Two Weeks Notice*, Dana Ivey, 2002, © Warner Brothers/courtesy Everett Collection.

p. 207: *Trouble with Normal*, David Krumholtz as Bob Wexler, 2000–present.

p. 208: *Back to Kansas (aka Married to the Kellys)*, Nancy Lenehan, 2003–04, © ABC/courtesy Everett Collection.

p. 210: *Drop Dead Gorgeous*, Sam McMurray, 1999. © New Line Cinema/courtesy Everett Collection.

p. 211: *Contender, The*. Robin Thomas, 2000.

p. 212: *Alice*, Celia Weston, 1976–85.

HEY! IT'S THAT CONVENIENTLY ORGANIZED, EASY REFERENCE

GUIDE!

THAT GUY?

LUIS GUZMAN!

The ARMY PAGE **14**

Adam **BALDWIN** PAGE **16**

Keith **DAVID** PAGE **17**

Zeljko **IVANEK** PAGE **21**

David **KEITH** PAGE **22**

John C. **McGINLEY** PAGE **23**

John
DIEHL

PAGE 18

R. Lee
ERMEY

PAGE 19

Michael
IRONSIDE

PAGE 20

Joe
MORTON

PAGE 24

Leland
ORSER

PAGE 25

Daniel
VON BARGEN

PAGE 26

The
BACKWOODS

PAGE **28**

HALL OF FAME
SEE PAGE 258

Joe Don
BAKER

PAGE **30**

Patrick
CRANSHAW

PAGE **32**

Courtney
GAINS

PAGE **38**

Clint
HOWARD

PAGE **39**

O-Lan
JONES

PAGE **40**

Brad
DOURIF

PAGE 33

Charles
DURNING

PAGE 34

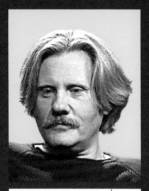

William
FORSYTHE

PAGE 36

John Carroll
LYNCH

PAGE 41

Tim Blake
NELSON

PAGE 42

Michael J.
POLLARD

PAGE 43

HALL OF FAME
SEE PAGE 25

Michael ROOKER | PAGE **41**

Tracey WALTER | PAGE **45**

The BIG CITY | PAGE **46**

Frances FISHER | PAGE **52**

Lee GARLINGTON | PAGE **53**

Adam GOLDBERG | PAGE **54**

Jane ADAMS | PAGE **48**

HALL OF FAME SEE PAGE 254

Christine BARANSKI | PAGE **49**

Jennifer COOLIDGE | PAGE **50**

Arye GROSS | PAGE **56**

Philip Seymour HOFFMAN | PAGE **57**

John C. REILLY | PAGE **58**

Isaiah
WASHINGTON | PAGE **60**

Victor
WONG | PAGE **61**

The
COURTROOM | PAGE **62**

Richard
JENKINS | PAGE **68**

Ron
LEIBMAN | PAGE **70**

Bruce
McGILL | PAGE **71**

Maury CHAYKIN | PAGE **64**

Tovah FELDSHUH | PAGE **65**

John HEARD | PAGE **66**

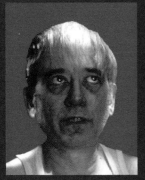

Austin PENDLETON | PAGE **72**

Oliver PLATT | PAGE **73**

Ron RIFKIN | PAGE **74**

Holland
TAYLOR

PAGE
75

The Gentlemen's
CLUB

PAGE
76

James
GANDOLFINI

PAGE
78

Frank
SIVERO

PAGE
83

Mike
STARR

PAGE
84

Aida
TURTURRO

PAGE
85

Michael
IMPERIOLI

PAGE 80

Debi
MAZAR

PAGE 81

Alex
ROCCO

PAGE 82

Frank
VINCENT

PAGE 86

Joe
VITERELLI

PAGE 87

The
GOVERNMENT

PAGE 88

| Xander **BERKELEY** | PAGE 90 | James **CROMWELL** | PAGE 91 | Bruce **DAVISON** | PAGE 92 |

| Donald **MOFFAT** | PAGE 96 | Will **PATTON** | PAGE 97 | James **REBHORN** | PAGE 98 |

Victor
GARBER | PAGE
93

Philip Baker
HALL | PAGE
94

Lucinda
JENNEY | PAGE
95

Saul
RUBINEK | PAGE
99

Fred
THOMPSON | PAGE
100

HALL OF FAME
SEE PAGE 255

J. T.
WALSH | PAGE
102

Harris
YULIN
PAGE
107

The
HIDEOUT
PAGE
104

Erick
AVARI
PAGE
106

Robert
DAVI
PAGE
111

Billy
DRAGO
PAGE
112

William
FICHTNER
PAGE
114

Sean
BEAN

Steve
BUSCEMI

Clifton
COLLINS JR.

Brendan
GLEESON

Jon
GRIES

Luis
GUZMAN

James
HONG
PAGE
118

Ricky
JAY
PAGE
119

Al
LEONG
PAGE
120

HALL OF FAME
SEE PAGE 255

Danny
TREJO
PAGE
124

The
HOSPITAL
PAGE
126

HALL OF FAME
SEE PAGE 255

Ellen **ALBERTINI**
DOW
PAGE
128

HEY! IT'S THAT CONVENIENTLY ORGANIZED, EASY REFERENCE GUIDE!

Delroy
LINDO

PAGE **121**

Peter
STORMARE

PAGE **122**

Brian
THOMPSON

PAGE **123**

Bruce
ALTMAN

PAGE **129**

Amy
AQUINO

PAGE **130**

Viola
DAVIS

PAGE **131**

Glenn
FITZGERALD

PAGE 132

Margo
MARTINDALE

PAGE 133

J. K.
SIMMONS

PAGE 134

Dylan
BAKER

PAGE 140

Gary
COLE

PAGE 142

Paul
GIAMATTI

PAGE 144

Stellan
SKARSGARD

Joey
SLOTNICK

The
OFFICE

Judy
GREER

Zach
GRENIER

John Michael
HIGGINS

Stephen ROOT | PAGE 150

Jay O. SANDERS | PAGE 151

Nick SEARCY | PAGE 152

Clancy BROWN | PAGE 157

George DZUNDZA | PAGE 158

Miguel FERRER | PAGE 160

HEY! IT'S THAT CONVENIENTLY ORGANIZED, EASY REFERENCE GUIDE!

HALL OF FAME
SEE PAGE 254

Stephen TOBOLOWSKY | PAGE **153**

The PRECINCT | PAGE **154**

Gary BASARABA | PAGE **156**

Paul GUILFOYLE | PAGE **161**

Ted LEVINE | PAGE **162**

Bill NUNN | PAGE **163**

Jon **POLITO** | PAGE 164

C. C. H. **POUNDER** | PAGE 166

The **SCHOOL** | PAGE 168

John **KAPELOS** | PAGE 174

Taryn **MANNING** | PAGE 175

HALL OF FAME
SEE PAGE 25

Edie **McCLURG** | PAGE 176

Troy
EVANS

PAGE
170

Paul
GLEASON

PAGE
171

Jeffrey
JONES

PAGE
172

Lochlyn
MUNRO

PAGE
177

HALL OF FAME
SEE PAGE 264

Vincent
SCHIAVELLI

PAGE
178

HALL OF FAME
SEE PAGE 264

Wallace
SHAWN

PAGE
179

Gedde
WATANABE

George
WYNER

The
STUDIO

Judah
FRIEDLANDER

Harriet Sansom
HARRIS

Christopher
McDONALD

William
ATHERTON

PAGE 184

Bob
BALABAN

PAGE 185

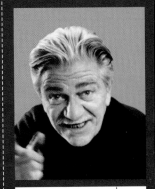

Seymour
CASSEL

PAGE 186

Larry
MILLER

PAGE 191

David
PAYMER

PAGE 192

Jeffrey
TAMBOR

PAGE 194

| Robert **WUHL** | PAGE **195** |

| The **SUBURBS** | PAGE **196** |

| Caroline **AARON** | PAGE **198** |

| Brian **DOYLE-MURRAY** | PAGE **202** |

| Bruce **GREENWOOD** | PAGE **203** |

| Dan **HEDAYA** | PAGE **204** |

**Kathy
BAKER**

PAGE
199

**Craig
BIERKO**

PAGE
200

**Paul
DOOLEY**

PAGE
201

**Dana
IVEY**

PAGE
206

**David
KRUMHOLTZ**

PAGE
207

**Nancy
LENEHAN**

PAGE
208

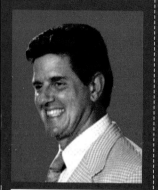

Sam
McMURRAY | PAGE **210**

Robin
THOMAS | PAGE **211**

Celia
WESTON | PAGE **212**

THAT GUY!

HALL OF FAME

Every actor we've profiled is a genius in his or her own right. But there are a few who've been working so long, so hard, or just so ubiquitously that we wish there were a Hey! It's That Guy! Hall of Fame, with interactive exhibits and a lavishly stocked gift shop where you could buy an Edie McClurg snow globe or a Stephen Tobolowsky commemorative spoon. Until that Hall of Fame exists as a physical location, however, this loving paper tribute will have to do.

Ellen
ALBERTINI DOW

PAGE
128

Joe Don
BAKER

PAGE
30

Christine
BARANSKI

PAGE
49

Edie
McCLURG

PAGE
176

Wallace
SHAWN

PAGE
179

Stephen
TOBOLOWSKY

PAGE
153

HEY! IT'S THAT CONVENIENTLY ORGANIZED, EASY REFERENCE GUIDE!

Michael
ROOKER

PAGE
44

Vincent
SCHIAVELLI

PAGE
178

Danny
TREJO

PAGE
124

J. T.
WALSH

PAGE
102

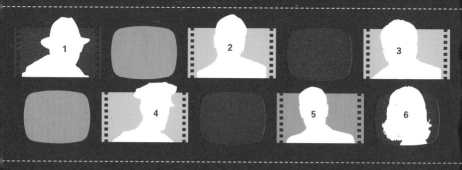

HEY! IT'S THAT FRONT COVER KEY!

1

2

3

4

5

6

7

8

9

10

11

12

13

14

15

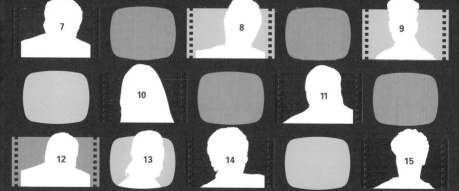